The Geste of the Great King

Office of the Passion
of
Francis of Assisi

Laurent GALLANT, OFM
André CIRINO, OFM

The Geste of the Great King

Office of the Passion
of
Francis of Assisi

The Franciscan Institute
Saint Bonaventure University
St. Bonaventure, New York
2001

The Geste of the Great King : Office of the Passion of Francis of Assisi / Laurent Gallant, André Cirino. – Saint Bonaventure (New York) : The Franciscan Institute, 2001. – 362 p. : ill.

Library of Congress Card Number: 00-110730

ISBN: 1-57659-175-1

1. Franciscan Sources 2. Liturgy

Copyright © 2001
The Franciscan Institute
Saint Bonaventure University
St. Bonaventure, New York 14778

Table of Contents

Preface	9
Foreword	13
Abbreviations	17

Section I: Praying hhe Little Office of the Passion

Introduction	21
The Geste of the Great King	22
The Hero's "Psalmic" Account of His Mission	23
A Window on Francis' Gospel Experience	
and on His Method of Contemplation	24
A Faith Vision of the World	26
How to Use This Little Office	28
How Francis Prayed His Little Office	28
Distribution of the Psalms of Francis	
During the Day and	
According to the Liturgical Seasons of the Year	29
1. Praying the Little Office Seven Times Daily	31
2. Praying the Little Office Three Tmes Daily	32
3. Praying the Little Office Twice Daily	33
4. Praying the Little Office Once Daily	34
A Note from the Translator	36
A Note from the Illustrators	37
Praying the Little Office	
Little Office with Psalm 1	41
Little Office with Psalm 2	47
Little Office with Psalm 3	53
Little Office with Psalm 4	59
Little Office with Psalm 5	65

Contents

Little Office with Psalm 6	73
Little Office with Psalm 7	81
Little Office with Psalm 8	89
Little Office with Psalm 9	95
Little Office with Psalm 10	103
Little Office with Psalm 11	109
Little Office with Psalm 12	115
Little Office with Psalm 13	121
Little Office with Psalm 14	127
Little Office with Psalm 15	133

Music

A Note from the Composer	139
Technical Indications	140
Symbols for Chanting the Little Office	140
Adaptation of Chords for Piano or Organ	141
Praises to Be Said at All The Hours	142
Refrain for Special Occasions	144
Prayer	144
Optional Choral Ending for Special Occasions	145
Antiphon	146
Without instrument	146
For piano, organ or guitar	148
Simple chant version	151
Psalms of Francis	153
Tones for Chanting the Psalms of Francis	153
1. For Ordinary Use	154
2. For Special Occasions	155
Psalm 1	156
Psalm 2	158

Contents

Psalm 3	160
Psalm 4	162
Psalm 5	164
Psalm 6	166
Psalm 7	168
Psalm 8	170
Psalm 9	172
Psalm 10	174
Psalm 11	176
Psalm 12	178
Psalm 13	180
Psalm 14	182
Psalm 15	184
Blessing–Dismissal	188
Without instrument	188
For piano, organ or guitar	189
For 3 voices	190

Section II: Commentary

Introduction	193
The Existing Collection	193
The Origin of This Collection of Texts	194
A Commemoration	195
A Nativity Song	197
Psalms in Honor of the Five Wounds	197
The Evolution Towards a Little Office	198
An Introduction	
to a Christian Reading of the Psalms	200
A Quatrain StructurePostlude	201
In Search of a Name	202
Remarks on the Translations of Scriptural Texts	
Used in This Work	203
Latin Insertions	204

Contents

About the Commentaries	205
Ordinary Components of the Office	207
Praises to Be Said at All the Hours	210
Antiphon	219
Blessing–Dismissal	223
Variable Components of the Office: The Psalms of Francis	225
Prelude	225
1st Series – The Main Theme: The Hero's Geste	227
Psalm 1	229
Psalm 2	237
Psalm 3	245
Psalm 4	250
Psalm 5	258
Psalm 6	269
Psalm 7	281
2nd Series – The Easter Variations	293
Psalm 8	294
Psalm 9	298
3rd Series – The Festive Variations	305
Psalm 10	307
Psalm 11	313
Psalm 12	320
4th Series – The Advent Motif	325
Psalm 13	326
Psalm 14	331
5th Series – The Christmas Motif	345
Psalm 15	346
Postlude	361

Preface

"How loudly I cried out to you, my God, as I read the psalms of David, songs full of faith, outbursts of devotion with no room in them for the breath of pride!... How loudly I began to cry out to you in those psalms, how I was inflamed by them with love for you and fired to recite them to the whole world, were I able, as a remedy against human pride!"[1] Thus does Augustine declare his reverence for the Psalter which anchors his new-found faith and opens his spirit to the depths of divine intimacy. Indeed, through all ages that have witnessed grace granted to mortals by the God of Abraham, the Father of Jesus, the psalms have been a beloved expression of that gift. We might even go so far as to say that this turn to the psalms as font of adoration and supplication is in itself a touchstone of authentic Judeo-Christian spirituality. Whether we look at Augustine praying in Cassiciacum or the American writer Kathleen Norris joining the monastic choir in Collegeville, we see the thread of the psalms woven through countless spiritual biographies.

It will come as no surprise, then, to realize that this book of Prayer was fundamental to the life of Francis of Assisi. Hailed as one of the truly original religious geniuses of the second millennium, Francis immersed himself in the psalms. There he found the assurance of praying precisely as Jesus himself once prayed and of fidelity to the Church which offered that prayer "without ceasing" by structuring its major liturgical actions around the psalms. In the twentieth century students of the spirituality of the Franciscan school published countless works exploring the sources of Francis' unique approach to union with Christ. Sometimes with artless simplicity, sometimes with rigorous investigation, admirers and scholars have searched for keys to interpret and to appropriate the power of his ecstatic intimacy with his God.

In spite of the fact that for nearly forty years we have possessed several trustworthy editions of his writings in English, we must admit that the *Office of the Passion* is one prayer text that has not received much attention. Here I hazard a guess as to the reason for this neglect. Until now, many of the students of Franciscan texts have come from within the ranks of professed religious. Their liturgical practice of recitation of the Divine Office or the Liturgy of the Hours is regulated by liturgical rubrics which confer a uniformity to the celebration of this prayer which is obligatory for many religious orders and institutes. Thanks to the vitality of post-counciliar liturgical reform this uniformity is not monolithic, but it does provide a model for observance that influences any conversation about alternative forms of a community's obligatory prayer practices.

For a generation of Franciscans schooled to this observance, the appearance of the English text of the Office of the Passion in early editions (the *Omnibus*, for example) offered a prayer form that appeared confusing in structure and rubrics. In spite of some excellent studies published by *Greyfriars Review*[2], our occasional attempts to pray the Office were often unsatisfactory. How to weigh its individual psalms designated also for various seasons of the year with the complete cycle presented in approved breviaries? – This was the question. Lacking answers and enjoying ample liturgical resources for use of the Psalter, the *Office of the Passion* languished on our shelves unknown and unsung.

With the publication of this new edition of the *Office of the Passion*, it is safe to predict that this unfortunate absence of understanding and enthusiasm is about to become a thing of the past. How many times in the pages of Franciscan history we discover that a changed practice or conviction can be traced to retrieval of authentic source material and the interpretations of those sources by experts? The team of collaborators who have worked to produce this edition bring to bear on the project an enviable combination of talents and proven dedication to the Franciscan tradition. Their contributions are outlined in the foreword.

The possibility of utilizing this Office as a form of personal and communal prayer offers all admirers of the early Franciscans a doorway into the inner world of their intense liturgical and biblical life. The distance that we lament between their ardor and our often frustrated attempts to adhere to the patterns they left us can be bridged by a work such as the one you now hold in your hands. However brilliantly we theorize about the tremendous unity of desire and purpose we see in these radical thirteenth century Christians, we theorize to our peril when we fail to make the connection between the Scriptural fonts and their daily life's choices. Making those connections as a matter of study, theological reflection or historical investigation has its value. Making those connections as a matter of lived praxis has its value. The *Office of the Passion*, now published in this edition founded on exhaustive research, musical and artistic harmonies, and intense collaborative effort, makes new connections possible. Let us rejoice in this gift. Let us pray…

Margaret Carney, OSF

---

[1] Augustine, *The Confessions*, trans. Maria Boulding, OSB, Vintage Books, New York, 1997, p. 175-76.
[2] See the work of Dominique Gagnan, *The Office of the Passion. The Daily Prayer of St. Francis of Assisi*, in Vol. 7 Supplement [1993] 1-89, for example.

Foreword

While browsing through one of the many bookstores on the *Via della Conciliazione* in Rome, I picked up an illustrated booklet of the *Office of the Passion* of St. Francis. From that day I began to dream of having such a publication available in English so as to make this prayer of Francis more accessible for people to pray.

My dream remained simply that until 1990 when I was facilitating a lengthy pilgrimage called "The Assisi Experience." One of the pilgrims from Montreal was Laurent Gallant, OFM. During the course of our conversations I learned that he had done his doctoral thesis in 1978 entitled *Dominus Regnavit A Ligno* (The Lord Has Reigned from the Wood) on the *Office of the Passion* at the Liturgical Institute of Paris. We soon discovered our mutual interest in this Little Office and decided to design a volume on this writing of Francis for prayer and reflection. To do so, we set out to draw from Gallant's very technical and lengthy thesis that material which would be of interest to a wider public. Thus the prayer book you have in hand!

The *Legend of St. Clare* states:

> She learned the Office of the Cross
> as Francis, the lover of the Cross, arranged it,
> and used it frequently with a similar fondness.

Both Francis and Clare prayed the *Office of the Passion*, she frequently and he daily, and yet, among Franciscans down through the centuries, the *Office of the Passion* seems to have fallen almost completely into disuse. Why?

One possible explanation is the fact that after St. Francis' death, St. Bonaventure composed a similar office for St. Louis IX, King of France. And because his office more closely resembled the regular form of the canonical office, it was utilized by many to the exclusion of Francis' composition. This neglect has prevailed into this century. For one rarely meets a Franciscan who knows much about the *Office of the Passion*, let alone how to pray it.

With the publication of new translations of the writings of St Francis in many languges, an awareness of the *Office of the Passion* among Franciscans and lovers of St. Francis has begun to emerge. And it is in light of this growing awareness that this prayer book is presented.

With the intention of creating an office book for prayer, we were interested in the possibility of singing the *Office of the Passion*. This has been made possible through the musical talent of Josef Raischl, SFO, who composed original melodies for the entire Little Office.

With the added aim of creating an office book for reflective prayer, two artists, Marcus Lisle and Christine Cavalier, were engaged to illuminate the manuscript, producing artistic linkages between the written text and the iconic text of the San Damiano Crucifix. This visual richness serves to remind us of the powerful interplay between an artistic image that moved Francis profoundly and the melodic poetry of Israel's psalms placed upon the lips of the Son of David and re-imagined by the Umbrian son of the troubadours. Their

FOREWORD

artistic work throughout the text invites all to "ponder these things" in their hearts."

After completing a literal translation of the psalms of Francis, we asked the Poor Clares of Greenville (South Carolina) to test this version with its accompanying music for several months. This translation, closely following Francis' original text, seemed awkward for praying and singing this Little Office. So Murray Bodo, OFM, was invited to take our translation and compose a version for prayer and song that would be poetic, graphic and inclusive. While attempting to employ inclusive language whenever possible in this prayer/song version, frequent references to the Father or to Jesus as the Lord have been retained to preserve the meaning of the original text.

So the result is two versions of the psalms of Francis:
1. for reflection and consideration, a literal translation faithful to Francis' original text as found in the commentaries on each component of this Little Office of St. Francis;
2. for praying or singing the Little Office, a translation that has moved from the more literal to the more literary.

The literal, though sometimes awkward, translation has been retained in the commentaries as a working text so that one can see not only how Francis uses the same words at different times, but also to convey something of the nuances he creates by using the same words in similar or contrasting situations.

With the objective of creating an office book for readability, the hidden work of Roberta McKelvie, OSF, our

Foreword

critical reader, laces the entire text. And the helpful advice and assistance of Michael Cervone bridged both the musical and computer worlds.

We owe profound gratitude to Robert Campagna, OFM, Provincial Minister of the Friars Minor Province of the Immaculate Conception, New York, for his interest in this project from its earliest stages. With his attentive advice, support and encouragement, the project has been able to advance through and beyond almost insurmountable hurdles.

Our appreciation also extends to Margaret Carney, OSF, Director of the Franciscan Institute at St. Bonaventure's University, not only for prefacing this work but also for her resolute desire to center this prayer once again in the heart of the Franciscan family.

And we gratefully acknowledge the talented computer expertise of Jean François Godet-Calogeras who readied this manuscript for printing by orchestrating it all – music, art, prayer forms and commentaries – into a coherent ensemble.

Finally, all translations of Scripture, writings of St. Francis and Franciscan sources are the authors' own.

André Robert Cirino, OFM

Abbreviations

1. Writings of Francis

Adm	Admonitions
ER	Earlier Rule *(Regula non bullata)*
LR	Later Rule *(Regula bullata)*
2LtF	Second Letter to the Faithful
LtOrd	Letter to the Entire Order
SalV	Salutation of Virtues
Test	Testament

2. Office of The Passion

Antiphon	Antiphon *Holy Virgin Mary*
Praises	Praises To Be Said At All The Hours
PsF	Psalms of Francis

3. Franciscan Sources

AC	Assisi Compilation (also known as The Legend of Perugia)
1C	First Life of Francis by Thomas of Celano
2C	Second Life of Francis by Thomas of Celano
LMj	Major Legend of Francis by St. Bonaventure
1MP	Mirror of Perfection, Larger Version

4. Others

Ps	Psalms
v.	verse
vv.	verses

SECTION ONE

PRAYING THE LITTLE OFFICE OF THE PASSION

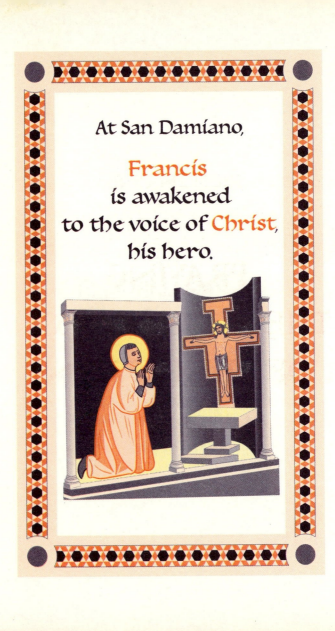

Introduction

"I am the herald of the great King!" answered Francis of Assisi to some robbers as they accosted him singing the praises of the Lord in the woods [1C 16]. The "great King" was, of course, Jesus Christ whom Francis had recently chosen as his "Lord and Teacher" and whose footsteps he had decided to follow. And listen to the Teacher and follow the Lord he certainly did, to the point of being transformed even physically into the image of the Crucified One. This final transformation took place shortly before he would joyfully welcome Sister Death as the one who would usher him into the glory of his risen Lord.

When one seeks the secret of Francis' astonishing gospel transformation, one invariably discovers that secret in his ceaseless striving to become a true disciple of Christ the Teacher. It is interesting to note that the word for disciple in Greek, the original language of the New Testament, also carries the sense of "student" or "learner." And to the very end, Francis remained a learner, a student of Christ, and on his deathbed could still say: "Let us begin, brothers, to serve the Lord God because up to now, we have made barely any or not enough progress in anything" [1C 103].

To nourish his discipleship, he strove to put into practice what he wrote to his brothers: "Incline the ear of your heart and listen to the voice of the Son of God" [LtOrd 5]. He even invented for himself a very original prayer form which would permit him to listen every day to the voice of the Son of God, his Teacher. This is the prayer which is commonly known as his *Office of the Passion*.

The Geste of the Great King

Each individual piece of Francis' Little Office is easily classified as a hymn, a psalm, an antiphon or a dismissal. But an attentive reader quickly realizes that these various compositions form an ensemble whose coherence goes far beyond the thematic organization of the best planned liturgical office. The category in which they best fit is that of the *medieval* geste.

In Francis' time, the geste was an extensive song or saga extolling the valor and the great deeds of a hero, such as King Arthur and his Knights of the Round Table. In his Little Office, Francis, the "Herald of the great King," sings of his Hero. And in the various texts of his office one can easily identify the essential components a geste:

a. the **hero** of whom the geste sings;
b. the **mission** with which the hero is entrusted and which leads him to perform acts of great valor;
c. the **enemies** the hero has to confront;
d. the hero's **victory**.

In Francis' geste the hero is, of course, Christ who is sent by the Father. His mission, which is never explicitly described, can, nevertheless, be inferred from the action. Francis' geste is to be read as a transcription of the "Glorious Passion" of our Lord Jesus Christ according to the gospel accounts, especially that of John. The mission, then, stands out as the overthrow of the evil "Prince of this world" who usurped dominion over God's realm, that is, God's creation.

Though the Enemy, the "Prince of this world," never appears personally on the scene, his presence looms in the background. The Enemy acts through those he has blinded and misled (the "enemies" in the psalms of Francis), as seen from the way the gospel presents the opposition mounted against Christ. This climaxes in Jn 8:40–41,44 where Jesus declares to his adversaries: "You are trying to kill me . . . and you are doing the works of your father. . . . You have the Devil as father, and it is the desires of your father you want to accomplish. He was a murderer from the beginning. . . . He is a liar and the father of lies." As for the "enemies," victims ensnared by the Enemy, Jesus will pray for them in his final hour: "Father, forgive them for they know not what they do" [Lk 23:34].

So the real confrontation takes place between the Hero and the Prince of this world. And as Christ affirms in Jn 12:31: "Now the Prince of this world will be thrown out." It is precisely at this point in the gospel account that Francis' geste picks up the action.

The Hero's "Psalmic" Account of His Mission

But Francis' account differs in at least two significant ways from that of the gospels. Whereas the gospels describe the action from the viewpoint of witnesses of

Christ's encounter with the forces of darkness, Francis has the victorious Hero himself give an account of his mission to the One who had entrusted him with it. So the Hero's narrative is addressed to the Father.

The second major difference between the gospels and Francis' geste resides in the fact that to compose the Hero's account, Francis draws very little material from the gospel texts themselves but relies primarily on the book of Psalms. This he does in accord with the traditional belief that in the psalms is found a prophetical foretelling of Christ's "glorious Passion." As an immediate model for this, Francis had the liturgy which regularly applies to Christ certain key verses of the psalms, especially during the Lenten/Passion and Easter seasons.

Finally, for his Little Office Francis selected psalmic verses that recalled the events of the gospel narratives, but his emphasis is definitely the spiritual experience of his Hero, in particular, his continuous relationship in prayer with the One who sent him, his most holy Father.

A Window on Francis' Gospel Experience and on His Method of Contemplation

Since he prayed his Little Office seven times daily, it is logical to conclude that this spiritual exercise would become a constant point of reference for his evangelical way of life. In turn, his personal experience of the

Introduction

Hero's message would guide him in his selection of the components he would gradually incorporate into this Little Office. It is, therefore, not difficult to foresee that this prayer would reflect some of the major aspects of the gospel way of life Francis proposes. This will occasionally be pointed out in the commentaries.

The *Office of the Passion* also suggests Francis' usual method of contemplating the saving mysteries of the Christian faith:

- first he evokes in the *Praises* the victorious Hero in the glory of the Father;
- then he recognizes in the *Antiphon* the glorified Hero as his "Lord and Teacher";
- finally, in his *Psalms* and in the repetition of the *Antiphon*, Francis listens to the Hero-Teacher indicate how, through his own experience, the way of total obedience to the Father's will in contradiction to the way of the "Prince of this world," leads, through opposition and persecution, to the fullness of life in the Kingdom where Christ, the Hero-Teacher, has entered once and for all.

One can observe that this way of proceeding from glory-to-cross-to-glory as a way of obedience inspires all of Francis' writings in which he speaks of Christ. He refers first to the glorious state either of the eternal, pre-existing Word or of the resurrected Christ, and then to the sufferings of the Passion.

A misleading image of Francis frequently depicts him at the foot of the cross, suggesting that the focus of his contemplation was the suffering Christ. Likewise, one can be misled by the biographers of Francis—even the earlier ones—who, in accord with the religious sensitivity of their day, generally insist only on Francis' compassionate contemplation of the cross. However, Francis' method of contemplation first focuses on the goal of gospel living and then on the road—which road includes the cross—leading to the fullness of life. This method is more likely in tune with today's religious sensitivity.

A Faith Vision of the World

The geste portrays the work of darkness, evil and death; but, more importantly, it proclaims the victory of light, good and life "in superabundance" [Jn 10:10]. Francis harbored no naiveté concerning the weight of sin, which burdens humankind's march in the search for fulfillment. A real, yet superficial, view of the situation of the world as he knew it revealed the apparent victory of darkness, evil and death. But out of his faith experience, Francis evolved into a deeper grasp of reality, thanks to which he discerned God's Spirit at work in all of creation, gently nudging it along in its transformation into the kingdom of God.

With the cross of Christ, the new Tree of Life, salvation had been irrevocably planted at the very heart of creation, at the center of the earth [PsF 7:3]. The disciples of the Hero, Francis among them, would now be witnesses of this "Good News" throughout the world. Acting out of this faith vision and treating the whole world as a saved, albeit sinful, reality, Francis revealed to the world its dignity of restored brotherhood and sisterhood in Christ, and offspring of the heavenly Father.

The leper, the living dead of Francis' time, was the most striking example of the outcast and marginalized within Christendom. Ever since the Lord had led him "among them" [Test 1], he made a place within society for these "Christian brothers" of his [AC 23]. For the Christian world, the Sultan was one of the most powerful symbols of its deadly enemies, and Francis viewed and treated him as a brother. Finally, all of creation found its place in the family of God; Francis could truly say: "brother sun," "sister moon," "brother wolf," "sister lark."

Day after day, as he prayed his Little Office, Francis heard his Hero recall: **Holy Father, zeal for your house has devoured me** [PsF 5:9]. This constant reminder certainly helped him grasp the full scope of the invitation he had heard in the little chapel of San Damiano: "Francis, go, repair my house which . . . is being totally destroyed . . . " [2C 10]. The house to be repaired was not only the material building, but the whole Church, and beyond it, all of humanity, and finally, all of creation. As he learned to see more vividly the destruction caused to God's house by the Enemy's maneuvers, he also learned to discern the signs of his Hero's irreversible victory.

Singing as it does of the cosmic clash between evil and good, darkness and light, death and life, Francis' geste of the great King most surely became a major daily reference for the daring, creative, and hope-filled actions which characterize his life.

How to Use This Little Office

How Francis Prayed His Little Office

From the information contained in the rubrics found in the manuscripts of the *Office of the Passion,* we can reconstruct the manner in which Francis prayed his Little Office as follows:

a. the *Our Father* and the short doxology *Glory to the Father…*;
b. the *Praises To Be Said at All the Hours* and its prayer *All Powerful, most holy…*;
c. the Antiphon *Holy Virgin Mary…*;
d. three psalms:
   • one in honor of the Virgin Mary;
   • one in honor of his private devotions, which could vary with the days of the week and the liturgical seasons of the year;
   • one "in reverence, memory and praise of the Passion of the Lord";
e. the Antiphon *Holy Virgin Mary…*;
f. the *Blessing-Dismissal*.

This sequence, except for the prayer said after the *Praises* (b) rather than before the final Blessing/dismissal (f), corresponds to the general outline of the Liturgy of Hours, even if the sequence lacks some of its standard features, such as the reading and its versicle/response.

From the rubrics one can conclude that Francis prayed this Little Office as an introduction or as a spiritual preparation to the Liturgy of Hours. It is not certain

How to Use This Little Office

which psalms Francis prayed in honor of the Virgin and for his private devotion (d), both of which were most likely taken directly from the book of Psalms. Fortunately, we do have all the other components of his Little Office. One can, therefore, propose the following order for praying Francis' Little Office today:

1. the *Our Father* and the short doxology *Glory to the Father…*;
2. the *Praises to Be Said at All the Hours* and its prayer *All Powerful, most holy…*;
3. the Antiphon *Holy Virgin Mary…*;
4. one of Francis' fifteen psalms;
5. the Antiphon *Holy Virgin Mary…*;
6. the *Blessing-Dismiss*al.

Distribution of the Psalms of Francis During the Day and According to the Liturgical Season of the Year

Francis prayed his Little Office seven times each day. Consequently he had forseen seven psalms for each day, one for each of the following hours:

- **Compline** — *Night Prayer* – before retiring for the night;
- **Matins-Lauds** — *Office of Readings-Morning Prayer* – as a vigil in the middle of the night, or can also be said in the early morning before breakfast;
- **Prime** — *Prayer before work* – early morning or after breakfast;

- **Terce** *Midmorning Prayer* – during a morning break;
- **Sext** *Midday Prayer* – about noon;
- **None** *Midafternoon Prayer* – during an afternoon break, about three o'clock;
- **Vespers** *Evening Prayer* – in the evening.

It is to be noted that the Liturgy of the Hours of each day begins on the preceding evening with Compline; for example, the Liturgy of the Hours for Good Friday begins on Holy Thursday at Compline.

To avoid the inconvenience of having to shift to another section for the ordinary or repeated components of the Little Office, each of the fifteen psalms has been inserted in a complete office format. Therefore, fifteen complete versions of the Little Office are offered in the following pages, one for each of Francis' psalms. These offices are preceded by four charts that indicate which Little Office is proposed for a specific prayer time according to the different liturgical seasons as well as the frequency with which one desires to pray Francis' Little Office.

The above-mentioned charts include a liturgical category called "Sundays and Major Feastdays." What can this title "Major Feastdays" refer to today? One may consider as such those days which the general and particular liturgical calendars identify as "feasts" or "solemnities." One who prays the Little Office privately could also celebrate some days which have personal liturgical significance, such as a patronal nameday or the anniversaries of one's baptism, marriage, religious vows or ordination.

How to Use This Little Office

1. For those who would pray the Little Office as Francis did seven times daily

Francis prayed the fifteen psalms of his Little Office according to the daily Liturgy of the Hours and the different liturgical seasons of the year, as illustrated in the following chart:

Liturgical Hours	Compline	Matins-Lauds	Prime	Terce	Sext	None	Vespers
Good Friday & Holy Saturday	1	2	3	4	5	6	7
Eastertime until Pentecost	8	9	3	9	9	9	7
Weekdays during Ordinary Time after Pentecost	1	2	3	4	5	6	7
Sundays & major Feastdays during Ordinary Time after Pentecost	8	9	3	10	11	12	7
Advent	13	14	3	10	11	12	7
Christmas	8	15	3	15	15	15	15
Weekdays during Ordinary Time after Christmas & Lent	1	2	3	4	5	6	7
Sundays & major Feastdays during Ordinary Time after Epiphany & during Lent	8	9	3	10	11	12	7

Praying the Little Office of the Passion

Those who do not have the possibility of seven prayer times may adopt one of the following daily rhythms with a suggested distribution of the psalms of Francis.

2. For those who would pray the Little Office three times daily

M=Morning; **N**=Noon; **E**=Evening

Liturgical Seasons		Monday	Tuesday	Wednesday	Thursday	Friday	Saturday	Sunday
Good Friday & Holy Saturday	M				1	5		
	N				2	6		
	E				4	7		
Eastertime until Pentecost	M	3	8	3	8	3	8	3
	N	9	9	9	9	9	9	9
	E	7	7	7	7	7	7	7
Ordinary Time after Pentecost (on major feastdays: Sunday PsF)	M	1	3	7	3	6	3	9
	N	2	5	1	4	7	5	10, 11 or 12
	E	4	6	2	5	1	6	7
Advent	M	13	3	7	3	12	3	11
	N	14	11	13	10	7	14	12
	E	10	12	14	11	13	10	7

How to Use This Little Office

Liturgical Seasons		Monday	Tuesday	Wednesday	Thursday	Friday	Saturday	Sunday
Christmas to Epiphany	M	3	3	3	3	3	3	3
	N	8	8	8	8	8	8	8
	E	15	15	15	15	15	15	15
Ordinary Time after Epiphany & during Lent (on major feastdays: Sunday PsF)	M	1	3	7	3	6	3	9
	N	2	5	1	4	7	5	10, 11 or 12
	E	4	6	2	5	1	6	7

3. For those who would pray the Little Office twice daily

M=Morning; **E**=Evening

Liturgical Seasons		Monday	Tuesday	Wednesday	Thursday	Friday	Saturday	Sunday
Good Friday & Holy Saturday	M					1	5	
	E					2	6	
Eastertime until Pentecost	M	9	9	3	9	3	9	9
	E	7	8	7	8	7	8	7

Praying the Little Office of the Passion

Liturgical Seasons		Monday	Tuesday	Wednesday	Thursday	Friday	Saturday	Sunday
Ordinary Time after Pentecost (on major feastdays: Sunday PsF)	M	1	3	5	7	2	5	9
	E	2	4	6	1	4	6	7
Advent	M	13	3	11	3	13	10	12
	E	14	10	12	7	14	11	7
Christmas to Epiphany	M	3	8	3	8	3	8	3
	E	15	15	15	15	15	15	15
Ordinary Time after Epiphany & during Lent (on major feastdays: Sunday PsF)	M	1	3	5	7	2	5	9
	E	2	4	6	1	4	6	7

4. For those who would pray the Little Office one time during a day

Liturgical Seasons	Monday	Tuesday	Wednesday	Thursday	Friday	Saturday	Sunday
Good Friday & Holy Saturday					5	6	
Eastertime until Pentecost	7	8	9	7	8	3	9

How to Use This Little Office

Liturgical Seasons	Monday	Tuesday	Wednesday	Thursday	Friday	Saturday	Sunday
Ordinary Time after Pentecost (on major feastdays: Sunday PsF)	1	2	3	4	5	6	7
Advent	13	14	10	11	12	3	7
Christmas to Epiphany	15	3	15	8	15	3	15
Ordinary Time after Epiphany & during Lent (on major feastdays: Sunday PsF)	1	2	3	4	5	6	7

For groups such as local fraternities of the Secular Franciscan Order who meet and pray together on the same day once or twice a month, they should not feel constrained always to use the same psalm given for that day in the above Chart. They could freely choose different psalms for their successive meetings. Some groups might even prefer to pray two or more psalms at each gathering. In all cases though, it would be advisable to choose their psalms among those assigned by Francis for the appropriate liturgical season.

A Note from the Translator

There is temerity, to be sure, and trembling, as well, in endeavoring to translate any sacred text. So, when I was asked to contribute to an English rendering of the psalms of St. Francis' *Office of the Passion*, I was doubly daunted and not a little challenged. Here were two texts that would give anyone pause: the Holy Psalms themselves and Francis' careful compilation of psalm texts to make new psalm-prayers that were personal and meaningful to him. Mercifully, I did not have to work with the Hebrew or Greek which would have resisted my limited knowledge of these languages. I could work with the Latin St. Francis himself worked with, and I could work in consort with scholars who are much more knowledgeable than I, both about Latin and about St. Francis' *Office of the Passion*. In the end, challenge and temerity won out over awe and timidity; and together with other contributors to this holy enterprise, we have come up with a text that we believe others will be able to pray as well as sing.

The most satisfying aspect of this project for me has been the collaborative nature of the venture: Franciscan women and men working together on a text dear to them, sharing insights, relinquishing at times their own view of how a word was to be translated; and in the yielding, discovering new resonances and meaning in a communally agreed upon rendering of the word. The

A Note

project became for me an image of Franciscan life today and how we are still sisters and brothers working and kneeling together before the sacred words our Holy Father Francis taught us to reverence, wherever we find them, "for in honoring words, you honor the Lord who spoke them" [LtOrd 36].

Murray Bodo, OFM

A Note from the Illustrators

We were walking along Via Del Colle, in Assisi, when Father André Cirino first told us of his plans for this collaborative project on the *Office of the Passion*. In the midst of our second visit to the historic spiritual home of St. Francis, we had already revisited the Basilica of Santa Chiara, and gazed up at the suspended Crucifix of San Damiano—the very same icon which spoke to Francis almost eight hundred years ago. But like so many of the hundreds of thousands of pilgrims who view this icon, our eyes rested upon it for only a few minutes from a distance, over the mass of other visitors, and then we let the tide of the crowd's movement usher us out of the chapel, onward toward more sight-seeing.

We now can see the great expanse that exists between sight-seeing and visual contemplation. As we worked at adapting the individual miniatures for this Little Office from detailed reproductions of the Crucifix of San Damiano, we began to appreciate the design and symbology of this icon. By spending time working with the individual painted figures and the gospel histories they illustrate, we developed a deeper appreciation for the message this crucifix shares. This remains one of the main reasons for including the color miniatures with this text—so that the prayerful reader can find the same private contemplative connection to the crucifix that St. Francis experienced while alone in the Church of San Damiano.

In adapting individual sections from the San Damiano Crucifix for the miniatures within this prayer book, we have endeavored to remain faithful to the original lines and brushstrokes of the unknown Umbrian artist who painted them. We hope that these miniatures, though small in scale, will grow in your heart and allow you to come closer to the feeling and understanding that St. Francis had for these figures.

The word "miniature" comes from the Latin *miniare*, meaning "to color with red." We have used red throughout all of the miniatures, and it is seen as blood, and the vital color of physical life. Gold or yellow shines from the divine level, and the dark blue, close to the spiritual color of purple, provides the strength and defining edges to all the figures.

The illuminations for the General Introduction and Psalm 15 are based on details from the frescoes of the life of St. Francis painted by Giotto (and his assistants) in the Basilica of San Francesco, Assisi. The line drawing which accompanies the *Praises to Be Said at All Hours*

A Note

is a simplified depiction of the ornate mosaic-decorated interior of the Basilica of Santa Prassede, in Rome.

May these printed lines and shapes of color resonate deeply for those who pray and contemplate this *Office of the Passion*.

Marcus Lisle
Christine Cavalier

Gethsemane

Our Father...
Glory...

Praises to Be Said at All the Hours

1. Holy, Holy, Holy Lord, God Almighty,
   You who are, who were and who are to come:
   — Let us praise and exalt God above all forever!

2. You are worthy, O Lord our God,
   to receive praise and glory, honor and blessing:
   — Let us praise and exalt God above all forever!

3. Worthy is the slain Lamb to receive power and divinity
   and wisdom and strength, honor, glory and blessing:
   — Let us praise and exalt God above all forever!

4. Let us bless the Father and the Son and the Holy Spirit:
   — Let us praise and exalt God above all forever!

*

Praying the Little Office of the Passion

5. All you works of the Lord, bless the Lord:
   — Let us praise and exalt God above all forever!

6. Give praise to our God, all you God's servants
   and you who fear God, the small and the great:
   — Let us praise and exalt God above all forever!

7. Let heaven and earth praise the glorious One:
   — Let us praise and exalt God above all forever!

8. And every creature in heaven and on the earth
   and under the earth,
   and the sea and everything in it:
   — Let us praise and exalt God above all forever!

*

9. Glory to the Father and the Son and the Holy Spirit:
   — Let us praise and exalt God above all forever!

10. As it was in the beginning, is now,
    and will be forever. Amen.
    — Let us praise and exalt God above all forever!

Prayer

Almighty, most holy
most high and supreme God,
all good,
supreme good,
totally good,
You Who alone are good,
may we give back to You
all praise,

Little Office with Psalm 1

all glory,
all grace,
all honor,
all blessing,
and all good.
So be it.
So be it.
Amen.

Antiphon

Holy Virgin Mary,
> There is no one like you born in the world among women,
> Daughter and Handmaid of the most high, sovereign King, the heavenly Father,
> Mother of our most holy Lord Jesus Christ,
> Spouse of the Holy Spirit.

Pray for us
> with St. Michael the archangel
> and with all the powers of the heavens
> and with all the saints
> together with your most holy beloved Son, Lord and Teacher.

Glory...

Psalm

(Christ the Hero addresses the Father.)

1. O God, I have given you an account of my life; you have recorded my tears.

2. All my enemies were conjuring
       evil thoughts against me;
   they took counsel together.

3. And they repaid me evil for good
   and hatred for my love.

4. What they should have loved me for
       became a cause to slander me;
   but I prayed:

*

5. "My holy Father, King of heaven and earth,
       be not far from me,
   for tribulation is near and there is no one to help me.

6. Let my enemies turn back, the day I call on you."
   I knew then that you are my God.

7. My friends and companions drew near
       and stood against me;
   my neighbors stayed far from me.

8. You kept my friends far from me,
   they made me their abomination;
   I was handed over and was not able to escape.

*

9. Holy Father, keep not your aid far from me;
   my God, see to my assistance!

10. Make haste to help me,
    Lord, God of my salvation!

    Glory...

Antiphon

Holy Virgin Mary,
> There is no one like you born in the world
> > among women,
> Daughter and Handmaid of the most high,
> > sovereign King, the heavenly Father,
> Mother of our most holy Lord Jesus Christ,
> Spouse of the Holy Spirit.

Pray for us
> with St. Michael the archangel
> and with all the powers of the heavens
> and with all the saints
> together with your most holy beloved Son,
> > Lord and Teacher.

Glory...

Blessing–Dismissal

V/ Let us bless the Lord, the living and true God.
R/ Let us always give back to God praise,
glory, honor, blessing and every good.

V/ Amen. Amen.
R/ So be it. So be it.

Encounter with the Sanhedrin

Our Father...
Glory...

Praises to Be Said at All the Hours

1. Holy, Holy, Holy Lord, God Almighty,
   You who are, who were and who are to come:
   — Let us praise and exalt God above all forever!

2. You are worthy, O Lord our God,
   to receive praise and glory, honor and blessing:
   — Let us praise and exalt God above all forever!

3. Worthy is the slain Lamb to receive power and divinity
   and wisdom and strength, honor, glory and blessing:
   — Let us praise and exalt God above all forever!

4. Let us bless the Father and the Son and the Holy Spirit:
   — Let us praise and exalt God above all forever!

*

Praying the Little Office of the Passion

5. All you works of the Lord, bless the Lord:
    — Let us praise and exalt God above all forever!

6. Give praise to our God, all you God's servants
    and you who fear God, the small and the great:
    — Let us praise and exalt God above all forever!

7. Let heaven and earth praise the glorious One:
    — Let us praise and exalt God above all forever!

8. And every creature in heaven and on the earth
    and under the earth,
    and the sea and everything in it:
    — Let us praise and exalt God above all forever!

*

9. Glory to the Father and the Son and the Holy Spirit:
    — Let us praise and exalt God above all forever!

10. As it was in the beginning, is now,
    and will be forever. Amen.
    — Let us praise and exalt God above all forever!

Prayer

Almighty, most holy
most high and supreme God,
all good,
supreme good,
totally good,
You Who alone are good,
may we give back to You
all praise,

Little Office with Psalm 2

>all glory,
>all grace,
>all honor,
>all blessing,
>and all good.
>So be it.
>So be it.
>Amen.

Antiphon

Holy Virgin Mary,
>There is no one like you born in the world among women,
>Daughter and Handmaid of the most high, sovereign King, the heavenly Father,
>Mother of our most holy Lord Jesus Christ,
>Spouse of the Holy Spirit.

Pray for us
>with St. Michael the archangel
>and with all the powers of the heavens
>and with all the saints
>together with your most holy beloved Son, Lord and Teacher.

Glory…

Psalm

(Christ the Hero addresses the Father.)

1. Lord, God of my salvation,
   day and night I cried out before you.

Praying the Little Office of the Passion

2. May my prayer enter into your sight;
   incline your ear to my request.

3. See to my soul and liberate it,
   because of my enemies all over me.

4. Since it is you who drew me from the womb,
   you my hope from my mother's breasts,
   from the womb I was thrust into you.

*

5. From my mother's womb you are my God;
   do not move away from me.

6. You know my disgrace and my confusion,
   and my reverence.

7. In your sight are all who trouble me;
   my heart expected disgrace and misery.

8. I looked for someone
   who would grieve together with me
   and there was no one;
   and for someone who would console me
   and I found no one.

*

9. O God, the wicked have risen against me,
   the synagogue of the mighty have sought my life;
   they have not placed you in their sight.

10. I have been numbered with those
    who go down into the pit;
    I have become as one without help,
    free, but among the dead.

LITTLE OFFICE WITH PSALM 2

11. You are my most holy Father,
    My King and my God.

12. Make haste to help me,
    Lord, God of my salvation!

    Glory...

Antiphon

Holy Virgin Mary,
> There is no one like you born in the world
>   among women,
> Daughter and Handmaid of the most high,
>   sovereign King, the heavenly Father,
> Mother of our most holy Lord Jesus Christ,
> Spouse of the Holy Spirit.

Pray for us
> with St. Michael the archangel
> and with all the powers of the heavens
> and with all the saints
> together with your most holy beloved Son,
>   Lord and Teacher.

Glory...

Blessing–Dismissal

V/ Let us bless the Lord, the living and true God.
R/ Let us always give back to God praise,
glory, honor, blessing and every good.

V/ Amen. Amen.
R/ So be it. So be it.

A Morning Interlude

Our Father...
Glory...

Praises to Be Said at All the Hours

1. Holy, Holy, Holy Lord, God Almighty,
   You who are, who were and who are to come:
   — Let us praise and exalt God above all forever!

2. You are worthy, O Lord our God,
   to receive praise and glory, honor and blessing:
   — Let us praise and exalt God above all forever!

3. Worthy is the slain Lamb to receive power and divinity
   and wisdom and strength, honor, glory and blessing:
   — Let us praise and exalt God above all forever!

4. Let us bless the Father and the Son and the Holy Spirit:
   — Let us praise and exalt God above all forever!

*

Praying the Little Office of the Passion

5. All you works of the Lord, bless the Lord:
   — Let us praise and exalt God above all forever!

6. Give praise to our God, all you God's servants
   and you who fear God, the small and the great:
   — Let us praise and exalt God above all forever!

7. Let heaven and earth praise the glorious One:
   — Let us praise and exalt God above all forever!

8. And every creature in heaven and on the earth
   and under the earth,
   and the sea and everything in it:
   — Let us praise and exalt God above all forever!

*

9. Glory to the Father and the Son and the Holy Spirit:
   — Let us praise and exalt God above all forever!

10. As it was in the beginning, is now,
    and will be forever. Amen.
    — Let us praise and exalt God above all forever!

Prayer

Almighty, most holy
most high and supreme God,
all good,
supreme good,
totally good,
You Who alone are good,
may we give back to You
all praise,

LITTLE OFFICE WITH PSALM 3

>all glory,
>all grace,
>all honor,
>all blessing,
>and all good.
>So be it.
>So be it.
>Amen.

Antiphon

Holy Virgin Mary,
>There is no one like you born in the world among women,
>Daughter and Handmaid of the most high, sovereign King, the heavenly Father,
>Mother of our most holy Lord Jesus Christ,
>Spouse of the Holy Spirit.

Pray for us
>with St. Michael the archangel
>and with all the powers of the heavens
>and with all the saints
>together with your most holy beloved Son, Lord and Teacher.

Glory…

Psalm

(Christ the Hero addresses the Father.)

1. Have mercy on me, O God, have mercy, for my soul trusts in you.

Praying the Little Office of the Passion

2. Shadow me beneath your wings of hope
   until iniquity passes by.

3. I will call to my Father most holy, most high,
   to God my benefactor.

4. God sent help from heaven and freed me,
   God disgraced those who trampled me.

*

5. God sent mercy and truth;
   God snatched my soul from my fiercest enemies,
   from those who hated me,
   who were confident against me.

6. They rigged a trap for my feet
   and they buckled my soul.

7. They dug a pit for me
   and into it they have fallen.

8. I am prepared, O God, my heart is ready,
   I will sing and chant a psalm.

*

9. Arise, my glory, arise psaltery and harp,
   I will arise at dawn.

10. I will confess you before peoples, O Lord,
    I will chant you a psalm among nations.

11. For your mercy has reached even to the heavens,
    and even to the clouds, your truth.

12. Be exalted above the heavens, O God,
    and over all the earth be your glory.

   Glory…

Antiphon

Holy Virgin Mary,
   There is no one like you born in the world
      among women,
   Daughter and Handmaid of the most high,
      sovereign King, the heavenly Father,
   Mother of our most holy Lord Jesus Christ,
   Spouse of the Holy Spirit.
Pray for us
   with St. Michael the archangel
   and with all the powers of the heavens
   and with all the saints
   together with your most holy beloved Son,
      Lord and Teacher.
Glory…

Blessing–Dismissal

V/ Let us bless the Lord, the living and true God.
R/ Let us always give back to God praise,
   glory, honor, blessing and every good.

V/ Amen. Amen.
R/ So be it. So be it.

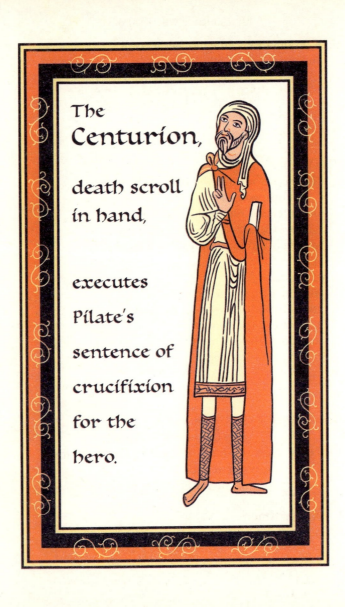

The **Centurion,** death scroll in hand, executes Pilate's sentence of crucifixion for the hero.

Encounter with the Imperial Authority

Our Father...
Glory...

Praises to Be Said at All the Hours

1. Holy, Holy, Holy Lord, God Almighty,
   You who are, who were and who are to come:
   — Let us praise and exalt God above all forever!

2. You are worthy, O Lord our God,
   to receive praise and glory, honor and blessing:
   — Let us praise and exalt God above all forever!

3. Worthy is the slain Lamb to receive power and divinity
   and wisdom and strength, honor, glory and blessing:
   — Let us praise and exalt God above all forever!

4. Let us bless the Father and the Son and the Holy Spirit:
   — Let us praise and exalt God above all forever!

*

PRAYING THE LITTLE OFFICE OF THE PASSION

5. All you works of the Lord, bless the Lord:
    — Let us praise and exalt God above all forever!

6. Give praise to our God, all you God's servants
    and you who fear God, the small and the great:
    — Let us praise and exalt God above all forever!

7. Let heaven and earth praise the glorious One:
    — Let us praise and exalt God above all forever!

8. And every creature in heaven and on the earth
    and under the earth,
    and the sea and everything in it:
    — Let us praise and exalt God above all forever!

*

9. Glory to the Father and the Son and the Holy Spirit:
    — Let us praise and exalt God above all forever!

10. As it was in the beginning, is now,
    and will be forever. Amen.
    — Let us praise and exalt God above all forever!

Prayer

> Almighty, most holy
> most high and supreme God,
> all good,
> supreme good,
> totally good,

Little Office with Psalm 4

You Who alone are good,
may we give back to You
all praise,
all glory,
all grace,
all honor,
all blessing,
and all good.
So be it.
So be it.
Amen.

Antiphon

Holy Virgin Mary,
> There is no one like you born in the world among women,
> Daughter and Handmaid of the most high, sovereign King, the heavenly Father,
> Mother of our most holy Lord Jesus Christ,
> Spouse of the Holy Spirit.

Pray for us
> with St. Michael the archangel
> and with all the powers of the heavens
> and with all the saints
> together with your most holy beloved Son, Lord and Teacher.

Glory...

PRAYING THE LITTLE OFFICE OF THE PASSION

Psalm

(Christ the Hero addresses the Father.)

1. Have mercy on me, O God,
    for all have trampled me underfoot;
    they oppressed me, attacking me all day long.

2. All day long my enemies have trampled me underfoot;
    how numerous those who have waged war against me.

3. All my enemies were against me,
    they were thinking evil things of me;
    they spread a hateful word about me.

4. Those who were guarding my life
    were scheming against me.

*

5. They were going outside
    and were plotting together.

6. All who saw me laughed at me;
    their lips spoke and their heads shook.

7. I am a worm, a non-human,
    a human disgrace, an outcast of the people.

8. Far more than all my enemies,
    I have become a total disgrace to my neighbors
    and a dread to my acquaintances.

*

Little Office with Psalm 4

9. Holy Father, keep not your aid far from me;
   my God, see to my assistance!

10. Make haste to help me,
    Lord, God of my salvation!

    Glory...

Antiphon

Holy Virgin Mary,
> There is no one like you born in the world
>   among women,
> Daughter and Handmaid of the most high,
>   sovereign King, the heavenly Father,
> Mother of our most holy Lord Jesus Christ,
> Spouse of the Holy Spirit.

Pray for us
> with St. Michael the archangel
> and with all the powers of the heavens
> and with all the saints
> together with your most holy beloved Son,
>   Lord and Teacher.

Glory...

Blessing–Dismissal

V/ Let us bless the Lord, the living and true God.
R/ Let us always give back to God praise,
    glory, honor, blessing and every good.

V/ Amen. Amen.
R/ So be it. So be it.

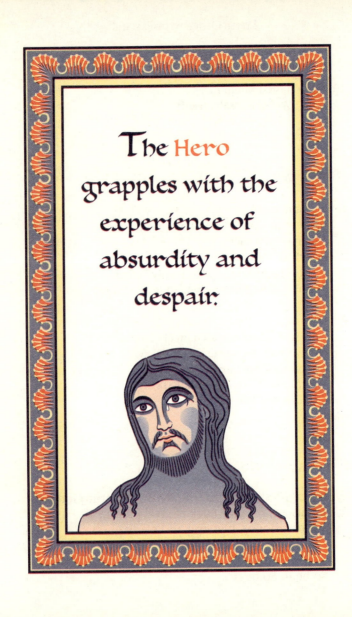

The Hero grapples with the experience of absurdity and despair.

On the Cross

Our Father...
Glory...

Praises to Be Said at All the Hours

1. Holy, Holy, Holy Lord, God Almighty,
   You who are, who were and who are to come:
   — Let us praise and exalt God above all forever!

2. You are worthy, O Lord our God,
   to receive praise and glory, honor and blessing:
   — Let us praise and exalt God above all forever!

3. Worthy is the slain Lamb to receive power and divinity
   and wisdom and strength, honor, glory and blessing:
   — Let us praise and exalt God above all forever!

4. Let us bless the Father and the Son and the Holy Spirit:
   — Let us praise and exalt God above all forever!

*

Praying the Little Office of the Passion

5. All you works of the Lord, bless the Lord:
   — Let us praise and exalt God above all forever!

6. Give praise to our God, all you God's servants
   and you who fear God, the small and the great:
   — Let us praise and exalt God above all forever!

7. Let heaven and earth praise the glorious One:
   — Let us praise and exalt God above all forever!

8. And every creature in heaven and on the earth
   and under the earth,
   and the sea and everything in it:
   — Let us praise and exalt God above all forever!

*

9. Glory to the Father and the Son and the Holy Spirit:
   — Let us praise and exalt God above all forever!

10. As it was in the beginning, is now,
    and will be forever. Amen.
    — Let us praise and exalt God above all forever!

Prayer

Almighty, most holy
most high and supreme God,
all good,
supreme good,
totally good,
You Who alone are good,
may we give back to You
all praise,

Little Office with Psalm 5

> all glory,
> all grace,
> all honor,
> all blessing,
> and all good.
> So be it.
> So be it.
> Amen.

Antiphon

Holy Virgin Mary,
> There is no one like you born in the world among women,
> Daughter and Handmaid of the most high, sovereign King, the heavenly Father,
> Mother of our most holy Lord Jesus Christ,
> Spouse of the Holy Spirit.

Pray for us
> with St. Michael the archangel
> and with all the powers of the heavens
> and with all the saints
> together with your most holy beloved Son, Lord and Teacher.

Glory...

Psalm

(Christ the Hero addresses Francis.)

1. With my voice I cried out to the Lord,
   with my voice I pleaded with the Lord.

2. In God's sight I poured out my prayer,
   before God the story of my troubles.

3. My spirit was failing within me,
   but you, you knew my paths.

4. On this road I was walking
   the arrogant have hidden a trap for me.

*

5. I looked to my right and saw
   that no one recognized me.

6. There is no escape;
   no one cares for my life.

7. Because of you I have endured disgrace,
   confusion has covered my face.

8. I became a stranger to my kin,
   and a pilgrim to my mother's children.

*

(Christ the Hero addresses the Father.)

9. Holy Father, zeal for your house has consumed me,
   and the abuses of your attackers have fallen on me.

10. They rejoiced and united against me;
    they scourged me and I knew not why.

11. They outnumber the hairs of my head,
    those who hate me without cause.

Little Office with Psalm 5

12. My enemies have been strengthened,
    those who persecuted me unjustly;
   they made me repay what I did not steal.

*

13. Evil witnesses rose up, questioned me
    on things I knew nothing about.

14. They were repaying me evil for good;
    they were slandering me for pursuing goodness.

15. You are my most holy Father,
    my king and my God.

16. Make haste to help me,
    Lord, God of my salvation!

    Glory...

Antiphon

Holy Virgin Mary,
   There is no one like you born in the world
      among women,
   Daughter and Handmaid of the most high,
      sovereign King, the heavenly Father,
   Mother of our most holy Lord Jesus Christ,
   Spouse of the Holy Spirit.
Pray for us
   with St. Michael the archangel
   and with all the powers of the heavens

and with all the saints
together with your most holy beloved Son,
> Lord and Teacher.

Glory...

Blessing–Dismissal

V/ Let us bless the Lord, the living and true God.
R/ Let us always give back to God praise,
> glory, honor, blessing and every good.

V/ Amen. Amen.
R/ So be it. So be it.

This icon, which Francis and Clare contemplated, proclaims the crucial experiences of the Hero's geste: his victory over death and his glorification.

Passage from This World to The Father

Our Father...
Glory...

Praises to Be Said at All the Hours

1. Holy, Holy, Holy Lord, God Almighty,
   You who are, who were and who are to come:
   — Let us praise and exalt God above all forever!

2. You are worthy, O Lord our God,
   to receive praise and glory, honor and blessing:
   — Let us praise and exalt God above all forever!

3. Worthy is the slain Lamb to receive power and divinity
   and wisdom and strength, honor, glory and blessing:
   — Let us praise and exalt God above all forever!

Praying the Little Office of the Passion

4. Let us bless the Father and the Son and the Holy Spirit:
   — Let us praise and exalt God above all forever!

*

5. All you works of the Lord, bless the Lord:
   — Let us praise and exalt God above all forever!

6. Give praise to our God, all you God's servants
   and you who fear God, the small and the great:
   — Let us praise and exalt God above all forever!

7. Let heaven and earth praise the glorious One:
   — Let us praise and exalt God above all forever!

8. And every creature in heaven and on the earth
   and under the earth,
   and the sea and everything in it:
   — Let us praise and exalt God above all forever!

*

9. Glory to the Father and the Son and the Holy Spirit:
   — Let us praise and exalt God above all forever!

10. As it was in the beginning, is now,
    and will be forever. Amen.
    — Let us praise and exalt God above all forever!

Prayer

> Almighty, most holy
> most high and supreme God,
> all good,

supreme good,
totally good,
You Who alone are good,
may we give back to You
all praise,
all glory,
all grace,
all honor,
all blessing,
and all good.
So be it.
So be it.
Amen.

Antiphon

Holy Virgin Mary,
> There is no one like you born in the world among women,
> Daughter and Handmaid of the most high, sovereign King, the heavenly Father,
> Mother of our most holy Lord Jesus Christ,
> Spouse of the Holy Spirit.

Pray for us
> with St. Michael the archangel
> and with all the powers of the heavens
> and with all the saints
> together with your most holy beloved Son, Lord and Teacher.

Glory…

Praying the Little Office of the Passion

Psalm

(Christ the Hero addresses the people.)

1. O you who pass along this way,
   look and see if there is a sorrow like mine.

2. For a pack of dogs has surrounded me
   a gang of evildoers has closed in on me.

3. Yes, they have stared at me and gloated;
   they have divided my clothes among them
   and have cast lots for my tunic.

4. They have pierced my hands and my feet;
   they have counted all my bones.

   *

5. They have opened their mouth against me
   like a ravening and roaring lion.

6. I have been poured out like water
   and all my bones have been pulled apart.

7. My heart has become like melting wax
   within my being.

8. My strength has dried up like baked clay
   my tongue has stuck to my palate.

   *

LITTLE OFFICE WITH PSALM 6

9. They have given me poison for my food
   and vinegar to slake my thirst.

10. They have led me into the dust of death;
    they have added to the pain of my wounds.

11. I have slept. . .and I have risen,
    and my most holy Father has received me with glory.

(Christ the Hero addresses the Father.)

12. Holy Father, You have held my right hand;
    you have drawn me by your will
    and have lifted me up with glory.

13. For what else is in heaven for me,
    and besides you, what have I wanted on earth?

(Christ the Hero addresses the people.)

14. Behold and see that I am God, says the Lord;
    supreme among the nations,
       supreme on the earth.

(Francis addresses the people.)

15. Blessed be the Lord, the God of Israel,
       who has redeemed the souls of his servants
       with his own most holy blood,
    and who will not abandon
       those who hope in the Lord.

16. And we know that the Lord is coming,
    and will come to judge justice.

    Glory…

Antiphon

Holy Virgin Mary,
> There is no one like you born in the world
> > among women,
> Daughter and Handmaid of the most high,
> > sovereign King, the heavenly Father,
> Mother of our most holy Lord Jesus Christ,
> Spouse of the Holy Spirit.

Pray for us
> with St. Michael the archangel
> and with all the powers of the heavens
> and with all the saints
> together with your most holy beloved Son,
> > Lord and Teacher.

Glory…

Blessing–Dismissal

V/ Let us bless the Lord, the living and true God.
R/ Let us always give back to God praise,
glory, honor, blessing and every good.

V/ Amen. Amen.
R/ So be it. So be it.

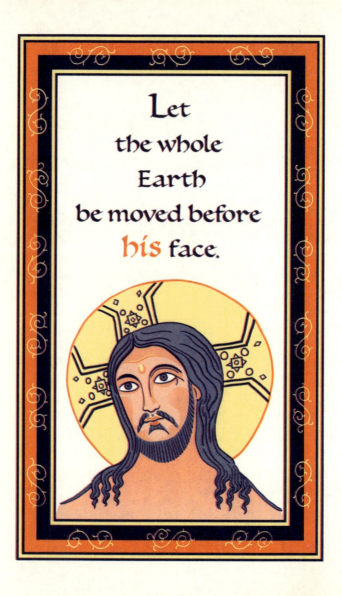

Acclamation of the Hero

Our Father...
Glory...

Praises to Be Said at All the Hours

1. Holy, Holy, Holy Lord, God Almighty,
   You who are, who were and who are to come:
   — Let us praise and exalt God above all forever!

2. You are worthy, O Lord our God,
   to receive praise and glory, honor and blessing:
   — Let us praise and exalt God above all forever!

3. Worthy is the slain Lamb to receive power and divinity
   and wisdom and strength, honor, glory and blessing:
   — Let us praise and exalt God above all forever!

4. Let us bless the Father and the Son and the Holy Spirit:
   — Let us praise and exalt God above all forever!

*

Praying the Little Office of the Passion

5. All you works of the Lord, bless the Lord:
   — Let us praise and exalt God above all forever!

6. Give praise to our God, all you God's servants
   and you who fear God, the small and the great:
   — Let us praise and exalt God above all forever!

7. Let heaven and earth praise the glorious One:
   — Let us praise and exalt God above all forever!

8. And every creature in heaven and on the earth
   and under the earth,
   and the sea and everything in it:
   — Let us praise and exalt God above all forever!

*

9. Glory to the Father and the Son and the Holy Spirit:
   — Let us praise and exalt God above all forever!

10. As it was in the beginning, is now,
    and will be forever. Amen.
    — Let us praise and exalt God above all forever!

Prayer

Almighty, most holy
most high and supreme God,
all good,
supreme good,
totally good,
You Who alone are good,
may we give back to You
all praise,

Little Office with Psalm 7

all glory,
all grace,
all honor,
all blessing,
and all good.
So be it.
So be it.
Amen.

Antiphon

Holy Virgin Mary,
> There is no one like you born in the world among women,
> Daughter and Handmaid of the most high, sovereign King, the heavenly Father,
> Mother of our most holy Lord Jesus Christ,
> Spouse of the Holy Spirit.

Pray for us
> with St. Michael the archangel
> and with all the powers of the heavens
> and with all the saints
> together with your most holy beloved Son, Lord and Teacher.

Glory…

Psalm

(Francis addresses the people.)

1. Clap your hands, all you peoples;
   raise to God a shout of exultation and joy.

2. Because the Lord is the Most High,
the awesome, great King over all the earth.

3. For the most holy Father of heaven,
    our King before all ages,
        sent the beloved Son from on high,
who planted salvation in the center of the earth.

4. Let heavens rejoice and earth exult,
let the sea and all that is in it roar,
let fields and everything in them sing for joy.

*

5. Sing a new song to the Lord;
all the earth sing to the Lord!

6. For the Lord is great and worthy of high praise;
worthy of awe above all gods.

7. Bring to the Lord, families of nations,
bring to the Lord glory and honor;
bring to the Lord the glory due his name.

8. Cast off the weight of sin
    and take up the Lord's holy cross;
and follow the Lord's most holy commands
    to the very end.

During Advent this psalm ends here.

*

9. Let the whole earth delight before the Lord's face;
say among nations:
    the Lord has reigned from the wood of a cross.

Little Office with Psalm 7

From Ascension to the beginning of Advent the following verses are added:

10. And the Lord ascended into heaven
    and is seated at the right hand
    of the most holy Father in heaven.

11. Be exalted above the heavens, O God;
    above all the earth be your glory.

12. And we know that the Lord is coming
    and will come to judge justice.

Glory...

Antiphon

Holy Virgin Mary,
> There is no one like you born in the world
> among women,
> Daughter and Handmaid of the most high,
> sovereign King, the heavenly Father,
> Mother of our most holy Lord Jesus Christ,
> Spouse of the Holy Spirit.

Pray for us
> with St. Michael the archangel
> and with all the powers of the heavens
> and with all the saints
> together with your most holy beloved Son,
> Lord and Teacher.

Glory...

Praying the Little Office of the Passion

Blessing–Dismissal

V/ Let us bless the Lord, the living and true God.
R/ Let us always give back to God praise,
   glory, honor, blessing and every good.

V/ Amen. Amen.
R/ So be it. So be it.

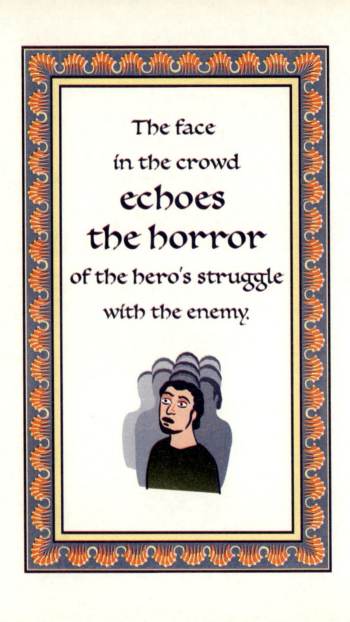

The face in the crowd **echoes the horror** of the hero's struggle with the enemy.

Echoes of Gethsemane

Our Father...
Glory...

Praises to Be Said at All the Hours

1. Holy, Holy, Holy Lord, God Almighty,
   You who are, who were and who are to come:
   — Let us praise and exalt God above all forever!

2. You are worthy, O Lord our God,
   to receive praise and glory, honor and blessing:
   — Let us praise and exalt God above all forever!

3. Worthy is the slain Lamb to receive power and divinity
   and wisdom and strength, honor, glory and blessing:
   — Let us praise and exalt God above all forever!

4. Let us bless the Father and the Son and the Holy Spirit:
   — Let us praise and exalt God above all forever!

*

5. All you works of the Lord, bless the Lord:
   — Let us praise and exalt God above all forever!

6. Give praise to our God, all you God's servants
   and you who fear God, the small and the great:
   — Let us praise and exalt God above all forever!

7. Let heaven and earth praise the glorious One:
   — Let us praise and exalt God above all forever!

8. And every creature in heaven and on the earth
   and under the earth,
   and the sea and everything in it:
   — Let us praise and exalt God above all forever!

*

9. Glory to the Father and the Son and the Holy Spirit:
   — Let us praise and exalt God above all forever!

10. As it was in the beginning, is now,
    and will be forever. Amen.
    — Let us praise and exalt God above all forever!

Prayer

Almighty, most holy
most high and supreme God,
all good,
supreme good,
totally good,
You Who alone are good,
may we give back to You
all praise,

Little Office with Psalm 8

> all glory,
> all grace,
> all honor,
> all blessing,
> and all good.
> So be it.
> So be it.
> Amen.

Antiphon

Holy Virgin Mary,
> There is no one like you born in the world among women,
> Daughter and Handmaid of the most high, sovereign King, the heavenly Father,
> Mother of our most holy Lord Jesus Christ,
> Spouse of the Holy Spirit.

Pray for us
> with St. Michael the archangel
> and with all the powers of the heavens
> and with all the saints
> together with your most holy beloved Son, Lord and Teacher.

Glory…

Psalm

(Christ the Hero addresses the Father.)

1. God, see to my assistance;
   Lord, hasten to help me.

2. May they be confounded and shamed,
   those who covet my soul.

3. May they be repelled and blush with shame,
   those who wish me evil.

4. May they retreat at once in shame
   those who jeer at me: Good! Well done!

*

5. But they who seek you,
   may they exult and rejoice in you,

6. And may lovers of your salvation repeat:
   May the Lord be magnified!

7. But as for me, I am needy and poor;
   O God, help me.

8. You are my helper, my liberator,
   Lord, do not delay.

   Glory...

Antiphon

Holy Virgin Mary,
> There is no one like you born in the world
> among women,
> Daughter and Handmaid of the most high,
> sovereign King, the heavenly Father,
> Mother of our most holy Lord Jesus Christ,
> Spouse of the Holy Spirit.

Little Office with Psalm 8

Pray for us
>with St. Michael the archangel
>and with all the powers of the heavens
>and with all the saints
>together with your most holy beloved Son,
>>Lord and Teacher.

Glory...

Blessing–Dismissal

V/ Let us bless the Lord, the living and true God.
R/ Let us always give back to God praise,
   glory, honor, blessing and every good.

V/ Amen. Amen.
R/ So be it. So be it.

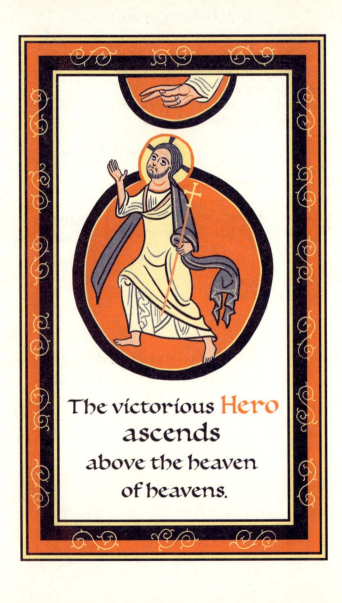

The victorious Hero ascends above the heaven of heavens.

The New Song

Our Father...
Glory...

Praises to Be Said at All the Hours

1. Holy, Holy, Holy Lord, God Almighty,
   You who are, who were and who are to come:
   — Let us praise and exalt God above all forever!

2. You are worthy, O Lord our God,
   to receive praise and glory, honor and blessing:
   — Let us praise and exalt God above all forever!

3. Worthy is the slain Lamb to receive power and divinity
   and wisdom and strength, honor, glory and blessing:
   — Let us praise and exalt God above all forever!

4. Let us bless the Father and the Son and the Holy Spirit:
   — Let us praise and exalt God above all forever!

*

Praying the Little Office of the Passion

5. All you works of the Lord, bless the Lord:
   — Let us praise and exalt God above all forever!

6. Give praise to our God, all you God's servants
   and you who fear God, the small and the great:
   — Let us praise and exalt God above all forever!

7. Let heaven and earth praise the glorious One:
   — Let us praise and exalt God above all forever!

8. And every creature in heaven and on the earth
   and under the earth,
   and the sea and everything in it:
   — Let us praise and exalt God above all forever!

*

9. Glory to the Father and the Son and the Holy Spirit:
   — Let us praise and exalt God above all forever!

10. As it was in the beginning, is now,
    and will be forever. Amen.
    — Let us praise and exalt God above all forever!

Prayer

Almighty, most holy
most high and supreme God,
all good,
supreme good,
totally good,
You Who alone are good,
may we give back to You
all praise,

all glory,
all grace,
all honor,
all blessing,
and all good.
So be it.
So be it.
Amen.

Antiphon

Holy Virgin Mary,
> There is no one like you born in the world among women,
> Daughter and Handmaid of the most high, sovereign King, the heavenly Father,
> Mother of our most holy Lord Jesus Christ,
> Spouse of the Holy Spirit.

Pray for us
> with St. Michael the archangel
> and with all the powers of the heavens
> and with all the saints
> together with your most holy beloved Son, Lord and Teacher.

Glory…

Psalm

(Francis addresses the people.)

1. Sing a new song to the Lord,
   the worker of wondrous deeds.

2. God's right hand and holy arm
   sacrificed the beloved Son.

3. The Lord made salvation known,
   revealed justice to the nations.

4. On that day the Lord sent mercy
   and song in the night.

*

5. This is the day the Lord has made;
   let us rejoice and be glad in it.

6. Blessed is the one who comes in the name of the Lord;
   the Lord is God, and has shone upon us.

7. Let the heavens rejoice and earth exult,
   let the sea and all that is in it roar,
   let the fields and everything in them sign for joy.

8. Bring to the Lord, families of nations,
   bring to the Lord glory and honor,
   bring to the Lord the glory due his name.

*

The following four verses are added:
- *on weekdays from the Ascension to the Octave of Pentecost;*
- *on Sundays and Major Feastdays from Ascension to Advent and from the Octave of Epiphany to Holy Thursday.*

9. Kingdoms of the earth sing to God,
   chant psalms to the Lord.

Little Office with Psalm 9

10. Chant psalms to the One
    who ascended to the East
    above the heaven of heavens.

11. Behold, God speaks with a voice of power;
    give glory to God, who governs Israel,
    whose splendor and power is on high.

12. God, wonderful in the saints,
    the very God of Israel,
    will give the people power and might.
    Blessed be God!

    Glory...

Antiphon

Holy Virgin Mary,
   There is no one like you born in the world
      among women,
   Daughter and Handmaid of the most high,
      sovereign King, the heavenly Father,
   Mother of our most holy Lord Jesus Christ,
   Spouse of the Holy Spirit.
Pray for us
   with St. Michael the archangel
   and with all the powers of the heavens
   and with all the saints
   together with your most holy beloved Son,
      Lord and Teacher.
Glory...

Blessing–Dismissal

V/ Let us bless the Lord, the living and true God.
R/ Let us always give back to God praise,
   glory, honor, blessing and every good.

V/ Amen. Amen.
R/ So be it. So be it.

A Shout of Joy

Our Father...
Glory...

Praises to Be Said at All the Hours

1. Holy, Holy, Holy Lord, God Almighty,
   You who are, who were and who are to come:
   — Let us praise and exalt God above all forever!

2. You are worthy, O Lord our God,
   to receive praise and glory, honor and blessing:
   — Let us praise and exalt God above all forever!

3. Worthy is the slain Lamb to receive power and divinity
   and wisdom and strength, honor, glory and blessing:
   — Let us praise and exalt God above all forever!

4. Let us bless the Father and the Son and the Holy Spirit:
   — Let us praise and exalt God above all forever!

*

5. All you works of the Lord, bless the Lord:
   — Let us praise and exalt God above all forever!

6. Give praise to our God, all you God's servants
   and you who fear God, the small and the great:
   — Let us praise and exalt God above all forever!

7. Let heaven and earth praise the glorious One:
   — Let us praise and exalt God above all forever!

8. And every creature in heaven and on the earth
   and under the earth,
   and the sea and everything in it:
   — Let us praise and exalt God above all forever!

*

9. Glory to the Father and the Son and the Holy Spirit:
   — Let us praise and exalt God above all forever!

10. As it was in the beginning, is now,
    and will be forever. Amen.
    — Let us praise and exalt God above all forever!

Prayer

Almighty, most holy
most high and supreme God,
all good,
supreme good,
totally good,
You Who alone are good,
may we give back to You
all praise,
all glory,

all grace,
all honor,
all blessing,
and all good.
So be it.
So be it.
Amen.

Antiphon

Holy Virgin Mary,
> There is no one like you born in the world among women,
> Daughter and Handmaid of the most high, sovereign King, the heavenly Father,
> Mother of our most holy Lord Jesus Christ,
> Spouse of the Holy Spirit.

Pray for us
> with St. Michael the archangel
> and with all the powers of the heavens
> and with all the saints
> together with your most holy beloved Son, Lord and Teacher.

Glory...

Psalm

(Francis to the people—to the whole earth.)

1. All the earth, shout joyfully to the Lord,
   chant a psalm to God's name;
   glorify God with praise.

2. Say to God: "How awesome are your deeds, O Lord;
confronted with your mighty strength
   your enemies shall recognize
   they have lied about you.

3. May all the earth adore you
   and sing psalms to you;
   may it chant a psalm to your name."

*

(Christ the Hero addresses the people.)

4. Come, listen, all you who fear God,
   and I will recount how much
       God has done for my soul.

5. I cried out to God with my mouth,
   high praise on my tongue.

6. And from the holy temple God heard my voice,
   my crying out in God's sight.

*

(Francis to the people—to the whole earth.)

7. Bless our God, you peoples,
   voice the sound of God's praise.

8. Every race on earth shall be blessed in God,
   and all nations shall magnify God.

9. Blessed be the Lord, the God of Israel
   who alone works wonders.

10. And blessed forever be God's glorious name,
    may the whole earth be filled with God's glory.
        Amen! Amen!

Glory…

Antiphon

Holy Virgin Mary,
    There is no one like you born in the world
        among women,
    Daughter and Handmaid of the most high,
        sovereign King, the heavenly Father,
    Mother of our most holy Lord Jesus Christ,
    Spouse of the Holy Spirit.
Pray for us
    with St. Michael the archangel
    and with all the powers of the heavens
    and with all the saints
    together with your most holy beloved Son,
        Lord and Teacher.
Glory…

Blessing–Dismissal

V/ Let us bless the Lord, the living and true God.
R/ Let us always give back to God praise,
    glory, honor, blessing and every good.

V/ Amen. Amen.
R/ So be it. So be it.

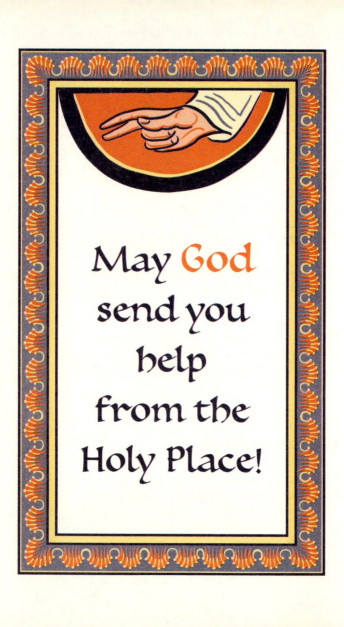

A Cry of Hope

Our Father...
Glory...

Praises to Be Said at All the Hours

1. Holy, Holy, Holy Lord, God Almighty,
   You who are, who were and who are to come:
   — Let us praise and exalt God above all forever!

2. You are worthy, O Lord our God,
   to receive praise and glory, honor and blessing:
   — Let us praise and exalt God above all forever!

3. Worthy is the slain Lamb to receive power and divinity
   and wisdom and strength, honor, glory and blessing:
   — Let us praise and exalt God above all forever!

4. Let us bless the Father and the Son and the Holy Spirit:
   — Let us praise and exalt God above all forever!

*

5. All you works of the Lord, bless the Lord:
   — Let us praise and exalt God above all forever!

6. Give praise to our God, all you God's servants
   and you who fear God, the small and the great:
   — Let us praise and exalt God above all forever!

7. Let heaven and earth praise the glorious One:
   — Let us praise and exalt God above all forever!

8. And every creature in heaven and on the earth
   and under the earth,
   and the sea and everything in it:
   — Let us praise and exalt God above all forever!

*

9. Glory to the Father and the Son and the Holy Spirit:
   — Let us praise and exalt God above all forever!

10. As it was in the beginning, is now,
    and will be forever. Amen.
    — Let us praise and exalt God above all forever!

Prayer

Almighty, most holy
most high and supreme God,
all good,
supreme good,
totally good,
You Who alone are good,
may we give back to You
all praise,
all glory,

all grace,
all honor,
all blessing,
and all good.
So be it.
So be it.
Amen.

Antiphon

Holy Virgin Mary,
> There is no one like you born in the world
> > among women,
> Daughter and Handmaid of the most high,
> > sovereign King, the heavenly Father,
> Mother of our most holy Lord Jesus Christ,
> Spouse of the Holy Spirit.

Pray for us
> with St. Michael the archangel
> and with all the powers of the heavens
> and with all the saints
> together with your most holy beloved Son,
> > Lord and Teacher.

Glory…

Psalm

(Francis addresses the Hero and then the people [6b, 7a, 8–9].)

1. May the Lord hear you in time of trouble;
   may the name of the God of Jacob protect you.

2. May God send you help from the holy place,
   and may God care for you from Zion.

3. May God be mindful of all your sacrifice,
   and may your burnt offerings be agreeable.

4. May God grant you your heart's desire,
   and fulfill your every plan.

*

5. We will rejoice in your victory,
   and in the name of our God we will be lifted up.

6. May the Lord grant all your requests.
   Now I have known that the Lord God
   sent the Son, Jesus Christ,
   who will judge the peoples with justice.

7. And the Lord has become a refuge for the poor,
   a helper in times of trouble;
   and may they, who have come to know your name,
   hope in you.

*

8. Blessed be the Lord my God,
   who has become my protector and refuge
   in my day of trouble.

9. O my helper, I will sing to you,
   for you, O God are my protector,
   my God, my mercy!

   Glory...

Little Office with Psalm 11

Antiphon

Holy Virgin Mary,
> There is no one like you born in the world
> > among women,
> Daughter and Handmaid of the most high,
> > sovereign King, the heavenly Father,
> Mother of our most holy Lord Jesus Christ,
> Spouse of the Holy Spirit.

Pray for us
> with St. Michael the archangel
> and with all the powers of the heavens
> and with all the saints
> together with your most holy beloved Son,
> > Lord and Teacher.

Glory…

Blessing–Dismissal

V/ Let us bless the Lord, the living and true God.
R/ Let us always give back to God praise,
glory, honor, blessing and every good.

V/ Amen. Amen.
R/ So be it. So be it.

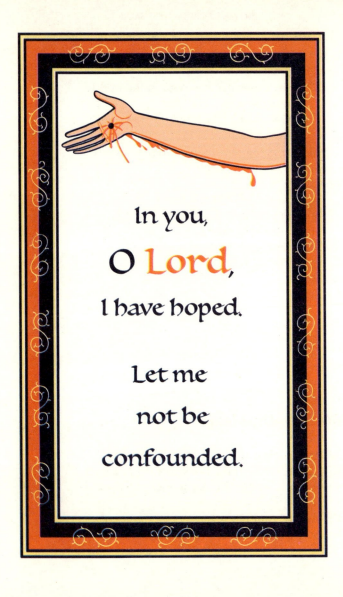

A Child's Prayer

Our Father...
Glory...

Praises to Be Said at All the Hours

1. Holy, Holy, Holy Lord, God Almighty,
   You who are, who were and who are to come:
   — Let us praise and exalt God above all forever!

2. You are worthy, O Lord our God,
   to receive praise and glory, honor and blessing:
   — Let us praise and exalt God above all forever!

3. Worthy is the slain Lamb to receive power and divinity
   and wisdom and strength, honor, glory and blessing:
   — Let us praise and exalt God above all forever!

4. Let us bless the Father and the Son and the Holy Spirit:
   — Let us praise and exalt God above all forever!

*

5. All you works of the Lord, bless the Lord:
   — Let us praise and exalt God above all forever!

6. Give praise to our God, all you God's servants
   and you who fear God, the small and the great:
   — Let us praise and exalt God above all forever!

7. Let heaven and earth praise the glorious One:
   — Let us praise and exalt God above all forever!

8. And every creature in heaven and on the earth
   and under the earth,
   and the sea and everything in it:
   — Let us praise and exalt God above all forever!

*

9. Glory to the Father and the Son and the Holy Spirit:
   — Let us praise and exalt God above all forever!

10. As it was in the beginning, is now,
    and will be forever. Amen.
    — Let us praise and exalt God above all forever!

Prayer

Almighty, most holy
most high and supreme God,
all good,
supreme good,
totally good,
You Who alone are good,
may we give back to You
all praise,
all glory,

Little Office with Psalm 12

> all grace,
> all honor,
> all blessing,
> and all good.
> So be it.
> So be it.
> Amen.

Antiphon

Holy Virgin Mary,
> There is no one like you born in the world among women,
> Daughter and Handmaid of the most high, sovereign King, the heavenly Father,
> Mother of our most holy Lord Jesus Christ,
> Spouse of the Holy Spirit.

Pray for us
> with St. Michael the archangel
> and with all the powers of the heavens
> and with all the saints
> together with your most holy beloved Son, Lord and Teacher.

Glory…

Psalm

(Christ the Hero addresses the Father.)

1. In you, O Lord, I have hoped
   let me not be shamed forever;
   in your justice deliver me, rescue me.

2. Be attentive to my call,
   and save me.

3. Be for me a protector-God and a fortress,
   keep me safe.

4. For you are my patience, O Lord,
   my hope since my childhood.

*

5. In you I have been strengthened from the womb,
   from my birth you are my protector;
   you will always be my song.

6. May my mouth be filled with praise
   that I may sing your glory,
   your greatness all day long.

7. Answer me, O Lord, for kind is your mercy;
   with the multitude of your mercies turn to me.

8. And turn not your face from your child;
   answer me quickly for I am in anguish.

*

9. Blessed be the Lord my God,
   who has become my protector and refuge
   in my day of trouble.

10. O my helper, I will sing to you,
    for you, O God are my protector,
    my God, my mercy!

    Glory...

Little Office with Psalm 12

Antiphon

Holy Virgin Mary,
> There is no one like you born in the world
> > among women,
>
> Daughter and Handmaid of the most high,
> > sovereign King, the heavenly Father,
>
> Mother of our most holy Lord Jesus Christ,
> Spouse of the Holy Spirit.

Pray for us
> with St. Michael the archangel
> and with all the powers of the heavens
> and with all the saints
> together with your most holy beloved Son,
> > Lord and Teacher.

Glory...

Blessing–Dismissal

V/ Let us bless the Lord, the living and true God.
R/ Let us always give back to God praise,
  glory, honor, blessing and every good.

V/ Amen. Amen.
R/ So be it. So be it.

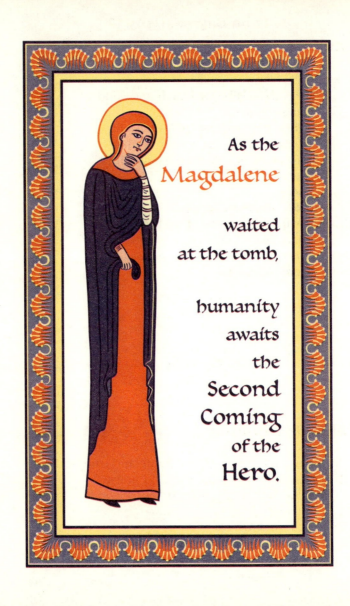

As the *Magdalene* waited at the tomb, humanity awaits the Second Coming of the Hero.

A Time of Expectation

Our Father...
Glory...

Praises to Be Said at All the Hours

1. Holy, Holy, Holy Lord, God Almighty,
   You who are, who were and who are to come:
   — Let us praise and exalt God above all forever!

2. You are worthy, O Lord our God,
   to receive praise and glory, honor and blessing:
   — Let us praise and exalt God above all forever!

3. Worthy is the slain Lamb to receive power and divinity
   and wisdom and strength, honor, glory and blessing:
   — Let us praise and exalt God above all forever!

4. Let us bless the Father and the Son and the Holy Spirit:
   — Let us praise and exalt God above all forever!

*

5. All you works of the Lord, bless the Lord:
   — Let us praise and exalt God above all forever!

6. Give praise to our God, all you God's servants
   and you who fear God, the small and the great:
   — Let us praise and exalt God above all forever!

7. Let heaven and earth praise the glorious One:
   — Let us praise and exalt God above all forever!

8. And every creature in heaven and on the earth
   and under the earth,
   and the sea and everything in it:
   — Let us praise and exalt God above all forever!

*

9. Glory to the Father and the Son and the Holy Spirit:
   — Let us praise and exalt God above all forever!

10. As it was in the beginning, is now,
    and will be forever. Amen.
    — Let us praise and exalt God above all forever!

Prayer

Almighty, most holy
most high and supreme God,
all good,
supreme good,
totally good,
You Who alone are good,
may we give back to You
all praise,

Little Office with Psalm 13

all glory,
all grace,
all honor,
all blessing,
and all good.
So be it.
So be it.
Amen.

Antiphon

Holy Virgin Mary,
> There is no one like you born in the world among women,
> Daughter and Handmaid of the most high, sovereign King, the heavenly Father,
> Mother of our most holy Lord Jesus Christ,
> Spouse of the Holy Spirit.

Pray for us
> with St. Michael the archangel
> and with all the powers of the heavens
> and with all the saints
> together with your most holy beloved Son, Lord and Teacher.

Glory…

Psalm

(Christ the Hero addresses the Father.)

1. How long, O Lord, in the end will you forget me?
   How long will you turn your face from me?

2. How long shall I bear conflict in my soul,
   pain in my heart all through the day?

3. How long will my enemy be victorious over me?
   Look at me and hear me, O Lord, my God.

4. Enlighten my eyes that I may not fall
       into death's sleep,
   that my enemy may never say: "I have prevailed."

*

5. Those who torment me would rejoice
       if I became troubled;
   but I hoped in your mercy.

6. My heart shall delight in your victory;
   I will sing to the Lord
       who granted good things to me,
   and I will sing to the name of the Lord, Most High.

   Glory...

Antiphon

Holy Virgin Mary,
   There is no one like you born in the world
       among women,
   Daughter and Handmaid of the most high,
       sovereign King, the heavenly Father,
   Mother of our most holy Lord Jesus Christ,
   Spouse of the Holy Spirit.

Little Office with Psalm 13

Pray for us
    with St. Michael the archangel
    and with all the powers of the heavens
    and with all the saints
    together with your most holy beloved Son,
        Lord and Teacher.
Glory…

Blessing–Dismissal

V/ Let us bless the Lord, the living and true God.
R/ Let us always give back to God praise,
    glory, honor, blessing and every good.

V/ Amen. Amen.
R/ So be it. So be it.

A Vision of Fulfillment

Our Father...
Glory...

Praises to Be Said at All the Hours

1. Holy, Holy, Holy Lord, God Almighty,
   You who are, who were and who are to come:
   — Let us praise and exalt God above all forever!

2. You are worthy, O Lord our God,
   to receive praise and glory, honor and blessing:
   — Let us praise and exalt God above all forever!

3. Worthy is the slain Lamb to receive power and divinity
   and wisdom and strength, honor, glory and blessing:
   — Let us praise and exalt God above all forever!

4. Let us bless the Father and the Son and the Holy Spirit:
   — Let us praise and exalt God above all forever!

*

Praying the Little Office of the Passion

5. All you works of the Lord, bless the Lord:
   — Let us praise and exalt God above all forever!

6. Give praise to our God, all you God's servants
   and you who fear God, the small and the great:
   — Let us praise and exalt God above all forever!

7. Let heaven and earth praise the glorious One:
   — Let us praise and exalt God above all forever!

8. And every creature in heaven and on the earth
   and under the earth,
   and the sea and everything in it:
   — Let us praise and exalt God above all forever!

*

9. Glory to the Father and the Son and the Holy Spirit:
   — Let us praise and exalt God above all forever!

10. As it was in the beginning, is now,
    and will be forever. Amen.
    — Let us praise and exalt God above all forever!

Prayer

Almighty, most holy
most high and supreme God,
all good,
supreme good,
totally good,
You Who alone are good,
may we give back to You
all praise,
all glory,

all grace,
all honor,
all blessing,
and all good.
So be it.
So be it.
Amen.

Antiphon

Holy Virgin Mary,
> There is no one like you born in the world among women,
> Daughter and Handmaid of the most high, sovereign King, the heavenly Father,
> Mother of our most holy Lord Jesus Christ,
> Spouse of the Holy Spirit.

Pray for us
> with St. Michael the archangel
> and with all the powers of the heavens
> and with all the saints
> together with your most holy beloved Son, Lord and Teacher.

Glory...

Psalm

(Christ the Hero addresses the Father.)

1. I will confess you, Lord, most holy Father,
    King of heaven and earth,
   for you have consoled me.

2. You are God, my Savior;
   I will act confidently and not be afraid.

3. You, O Lord, are my strength and my praise,
   you have become my salvation.

4. Your right hand, O Lord, is magnificent strength,
   your right hand, O Lord, has struck the enemy;
   and in your great glory
   >you deposed my adversaries.

*

(Francis addresses the people.)

5. Let the poor see and rejoice;
   seek the Lord and your soul will live.

6. For the Lord heard the poor,
   and has not scorned those captive.

*

7. Let heaven and earth praise God,
   the seas and all that moves in them.

8. For God will secure Zion,
   and the cities of Judah will be rebuilt.

9. And the poor will dwell there,
   and will inherit Zion.

10. And the descendants of God's servants will possess it
    and those who love God's name will live in it.

    Glory…

Little Office with Psalm 14

Antiphon

Holy Virgin Mary,
> There is no one like you born in the world
> > among women,
> Daughter and Handmaid of the most high,
> > sovereign King, the heavenly Father,
> Mother of our most holy Lord Jesus Christ,
> Spouse of the Holy Spirit.

Pray for us
> with St. Michael the archangel
> and with all the powers of the heavens
> and with all the saints
> together with your most holy beloved Son,
> > Lord and Teacher.

Glory…

Blessing–Dismissal

V/ Let us bless the Lord, the living and true God.
R/ Let us always give back to God praise,
glory, honor, blessing and every good.

V/ Amen. Amen.
R/ So be it. So be it.

Let the heavens rejoice,
and the Earth exult,
the sea
and all that is in it
be moved !
Let the fields
and all that is in them
be glad !

The Hero's Origin and Birth

Our Father...
Glory...

Praises to Be Said at All the Hours

1. Holy, Holy, Holy Lord, God Almighty,
   You who are, who were and who are to come:
   — Let us praise and exalt God above all forever!

2. You are worthy, O Lord our God,
   to receive praise and glory, honor and blessing:
   — Let us praise and exalt God above all forever!

3. Worthy is the slain Lamb to receive power and divinity
   and wisdom and strength, honor, glory and blessing:
   — Let us praise and exalt God above all forever!

4. Let us bless the Father and the Son and the Holy Spirit:
   — Let us praise and exalt God above all forever!

*

Praying the Little Office of the Passion

5. All you works of the Lord, bless the Lord:
   — Let us praise and exalt God above all forever!

6. Give praise to our God, all you God's servants
   and you who fear God, the small and the great:
   — Let us praise and exalt God above all forever!

7. Let heaven and earth praise the glorious One:
   — Let us praise and exalt God above all forever!

8. And every creature in heaven and on the earth
   and under the earth,
   and the sea and everything in it:
   — Let us praise and exalt God above all forever!

*

9. Glory to the Father and the Son and the Holy Spirit:
   — Let us praise and exalt God above all forever!

10. As it was in the beginning, is now,
    and will be forever. Amen.
    — Let us praise and exalt God above all forever!

Prayer

>Almighty, most holy
>most high and supreme God,
>all good,
>supreme good,
>totally good,
>You Who alone are good,
>may we give back to You
>all praise,
>all glory,

Little Office with Psalm 15

> all grace,
> all honor,
> all blessing,
> and all good.
> So be it.
> So be it.
> Amen.

Antiphon

Holy Virgin Mary,
> There is no one like you born in the world
> > among women,
> Daughter and Handmaid of the most high,
> > sovereign King, the heavenly Father,
> Mother of our most holy Lord Jesus Christ,
> Spouse of the Holy Spirit.

Pray for us
> with St. Michael the archangel
> and with all the powers of the heavens
> and with all the saints
> together with your most holy beloved Son,
> > Lord and Teacher.

Glory…

Psalm

(Francis addresses the people.)

1. Sing for joy to God our help;
   with exultant voice
   > raise to the Lord God living and true
   > a shout of joy.

Praying the Little Office of the Passion

2. Because the Lord is the Most High,
   the awesome, great King over all the earth.

3. For the most holy Father of heaven,
   > our King before all ages,
   sent from on high the beloved Son
   > who was born of the Blessed Virgin, Holy Mary.

4. He called out to God: You are my Father,
   and God placed him as the firstborn,
   > the highest above all earthly kings.

*

5. On that day the Lord sent mercy
   and song in the night.

6. This is the day the Lord has made;
   let us rejoice in it and be glad.

7. For to us is given the beloved child most holy,
   born for us along the way and placed in a manger
   because there was no room for him at the inn.

8. Glory to the Lord God in the highest
   and on earth peace to those of good will.

*

9. Let heavens rejoice and earth exult,
   let the sea and all that is in it roar,
   let fields and everything in them sing for joy

10. Sing to the Lord a new song;
    sing to the Lord, all the earth!

Little Office with Psalm 15

11. For the Lord is great and highly to be praised;
    more awesome than all gods.

12. Bring to the Lord, families of nations,
    bring to the Lord glory and honor,
    bring to the Lord the glory due his name.

*

13. Cast off the weight of sin
       and take up the Lord's holy cross,
    follow the Lord's most holy commands to the very end.

    Glory...

Antiphon

Holy Virgin Mary,
   There is no one like you born in the world
      among women,
   Daughter and Handmaid of the most high,
      sovereign King, the heavenly Father,
   Mother of our most holy Lord Jesus Christ,
   Spouse of the Holy Spirit.
Pray for us
   with St. Michael the archangel
   and with all the powers of the heavens
   and with all the saints
   together with your most holy beloved Son,
      Lord and Teacher.
Glory...

Blessing–Dismissal

V/ Let us bless the Lord, the living and true God.
R/ Let us always give back to God praise,
glory, honor, blessing and every good.

V/ Amen. Amen.
R/ So be it. So be it.

A Note from the Composer

Francis of Assisi was a lover of music and song. His biographers relate that in his younger days, he used to sing in the French dialect, Provençal [2C 127 and LMj 2:5]. It was through song that he expressed his feelings. And later on, singing became for Francis his most powerful means of praising God. Although he composed songs himself, unfortunately none of his melodies have survived. However, we do have his *Canticle of Brother Sun* (also called *Canticle of the Creatures*) and the *Canticle of Exhortation* that he composed for Clare and her sisters at San Damiano.

Francis believed in the reconciling, healing power of the sound of music and of the sung words. He sent his brothers to sing his *Canticle of Brother Sun* to the mayor and bishop of Assisi who were feuding. It was the power of the sound of song expressing his poetical verses that brought reconciliation and healing to the two men [AC 44 and 2MP 101].

Singing is not just a means for producing sounds, but can help to give rise to a powerful encounter with God. It is through song that one can express the feelings of the heart—love and praise, sorrow and anguish, desire and despair, hope and faith.

So it is because Francis loved music and song and used them to express the experiences of his heart, that the opportunity to sing his *Office of the Passion* is made possible.

Josef Raischl, SFO

Technical Indications

Symbols for Chanting the Little Office

__   The underlined syllable indicates a change of melody within the verse and the note which is underlined shows when the change is made.

/   The diagonal indicates a short pause without a change of note, except psalm tone 2.

[•]   The brackets surrounding a note in Tone 2 indicate a flex—a short pause within the first half of a verse and a change of note. The syllable and note are underlined. After the flex return to the dominant note. This occurs in psalms of Francis 2, 11 and 15.

|o| The double vertical lines surrounding a note indicate that the number of syllables sung on this note is not fixed.

Technical Indications

|•| The darkened note stands for one to four sung syllables.

*   The asterisk indicates a break or pause within the verse by taking a short breath.

V/ R/   The text of the Prayer and Antiphon can be alternated by a leader (presider or soloist) and all the participants. Their respective sections are traditionally identified by the letters V (leader) and R (all).

Adaptation of chords for piano or organ

Chords for the guitar are given with the psalm tones and other music. The chords should be adapted for the use of piano or organ as follows:

Bm7	B minor including the minor 7th [B D F# A]
Gadd9	G major including the 9th [G B D A]
E7add4	E major including the dominant 7th and the 4th [E G# A B D E]
E/D	E major with a D bass
Dmaj7	D major including major 7th [D F# A C#].

Praises to Be Said at All the Hours

1. Holy, Holy, Holy / Lord, God Almighty, *
   You who are, who were and who are to come:

Refrain:

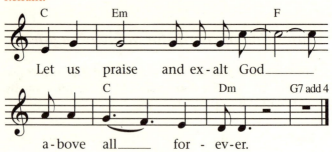

Let us praise and exalt God above all forever.

2. You are worthy, O Lord our God, *
   to receive praise and glory, honor and blessing:

Refrain: **Let us praise and exalt God above all forever!**

3. Worthy is the slain Lamb /
   to receive power and divinity *
   and wisdom and strength, / honor, glory and blessing:

Refrain: **Let us praise and exalt God above all forever!**

Praises to Be Said at All the Hours

4. Let us <u>bless </u>the Father *
   and the <u>Son</u> and the <u>Ho</u>ly Spirit:

Refrain: **Let us praise and exalt God above all forever!**

5. All you works <u>of</u> the Lord, *
   <u>bless</u> the Lord:

Refrain: **Let us praise and exalt God above all forever!**

6. Give praise to our God, all <u>you</u> God's servants *
   and you who fear <u>God</u>, / the small <u>and</u> the great:

Refrain: **Let us praise and exalt God above all forever!**

7. Let heav<u>en</u> and earth *
   <u>praise</u> the glor<u>i</u>ous One:

Refrain: **Let us praise and exalt God above all forever!**

8. And every creature in heaven and <u>on</u> the earth *
   and under the earth, and the <u>sea</u> and every<u>thing</u> in it:

Refrain: **Let us praise and exalt God above all forever!**

9. Glory to the Father and <u>to</u> the Son *
   and <u>to</u> the <u>Ho</u>ly Spirit:

Refrain: **Let us praise and exalt God above all forever!**

10. As it was in the begin<u>ning</u>, is now, *
    and will <u>be</u> for<u>ev</u>er. Amen.

Refrain: **Let us praise and exalt God above all forever!**

Refrain for special occasions

Prayer

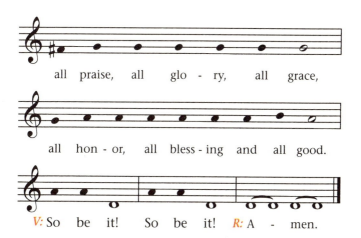

Optional choral ending for special occasions

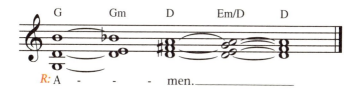

Antiphon

Without instruments

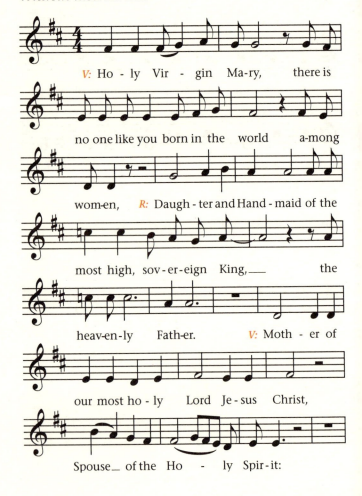

V: Holy Virgin Mary, there is no one like you born in the world among women, R: Daughter and Handmaid of the most high, sovereign King, the heavenly Father. V: Mother of our most holy Lord Jesus Christ, Spouse of the Holy Spirit:

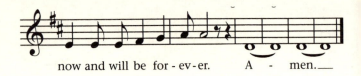

now and will be for-ev-er. A - men.

For piano, organ or guitar

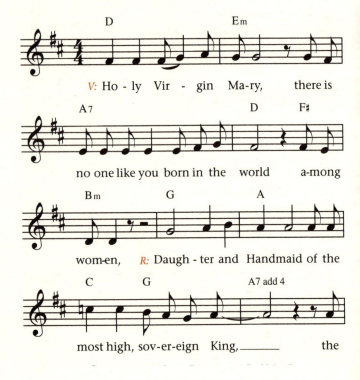

V: Ho-ly Vir-gin Ma-ry, there is no one like you born in the world a-mong wom-en, R: Daugh-ter and Handmaid of the most high, sov-er-eign King, the

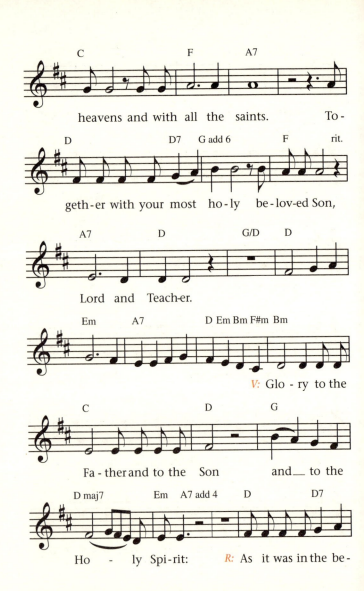

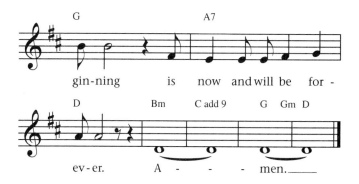

Simple chant version

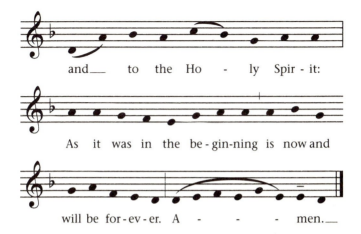

Psalms of Francis

Tones for Chanting the Psalms of Francis

There are five different tones composed for the Psalms of Francis and can be used as follows:

- Tone 1   Psalms of Francis 1, 4, 13;
- Tone 2   Psalms of Francis 2, 11, 15;
- Tone 3   Psalms of Francis 3, 5, 9;
- Tone 4   Psalms of Francis 7, 10, 14, 15;
- Tone 5   Psalms of Francis 6, 8, 12.

Tones for ordinary use

Tone 1

Tone 2

Tone 3

Tone 4

Tone 5

Tones for special occasions

For special occasions one can chant the psalms alternating between the congregation and a choir. The choir would start chanting the first verse in the simple psalm tone. The next part is chanted by the congregation. The second time the choir can break into three voices.

Tone 1

Tone 2

Tone 3

Tone 4

Tone 5

Psalm One

[Tone 1]

[For special occasion, see p. 155.]

(Christ the Hero addresses the Father.)

1. O God, / I have given you an account of <u>my</u> life; *
   you have record<u>ed</u> my tears.

2. All my enemies were conjuring evil thoughts <u>a</u>gainst me; *
   they took coun<u>sel</u> together.

3. And they repaid me evil <u>for</u> good *
   and hatred <u>for</u> my love.

4. What they should have loved <u>me</u> for *
   became a cause to slander me; / <u>but</u> I prayed:

5. "My holy Father, / King of heaven and earth, / be not far <u>from</u> me, *
   for tribulation is near / and there is no <u>one</u> to help me.

6. Let my enemies turn back, the day I call <u>on</u> you." *
   I knew then that you <u>are</u> my God.

7. My friends and companions drew near and stood <u>a</u>gainst me; *
   my neighbors stayed <u>far</u> from me.

Psalm 1

8. You kept my friends far from me, /
   they made me their abomi_na_tion; *
   I was handed over and was not able _to_ escape.

9. Holy Father, / keep not your aid far _from_ me; *
   my God, / see to _my_ assistance!

10. Make haste _to_ help me, *
    Lord, God of _my_ salvation!

11. Glory to the Father and to _the_ Son *
    and to the _Ho_ly Spirit.

12. As it was in the beginning, _is_ now, *
    and will be for_ev_er. Amen.

Psalm Two

[Tone 2]

[For special occasion, see p. 155.]

(Christ the Hero addresses the Father.)

1. Lord, God of <u>my</u> salvation, *
   day and night I cried <u>out</u> before you.

2. May my prayer enter in<u>to</u> your sight; *
   incline your ear to <u>my</u> request.

3. See to my soul and <u>lib</u>erate it, *
   because of my enemies all <u>o</u>ver me.

4. Since it is you who drew me from the <u>womb</u>, /
   you my hope from my <u>moth</u>er's breasts, *
   from the womb I was thrust in<u>to</u> you.

5. From my mother's womb you <u>are</u> my God; *
   do not move a<u>way</u> from me.

6. You know <u>my</u> disgrace *
   and my confusion, / <u>and</u> my reverence.

7. In your sight are all who <u>trou</u>ble me; *
   my heart expected dis<u>grace</u> and misery.

Psalm 2

8. I looked for someone
   who would grieve together with <u>me</u> /
   and <u>there</u> was no one; *
   and for someone who would console me /
   and <u>I</u> found no one.

9. O God, the wicked have risen against <u>me</u> /
   the synagogue of the mighty have <u>sought</u> my life; *
   they have not placed you <u>in</u> their sight.

10. I have been numbered with those who go down in<u>to</u> the pit; *
    I have become as one without help, /
    free, but a<u>mong</u> the dead.

11. You are my most <u>ho</u>ly Father, *
    My King <u>and</u> my God.

12. Make <u>haste</u> to help me, *
    Lord, God of <u>my</u> salvation!

13. Glory to the Father and <u>to</u> the Son *
    and to the <u>Holy</u> Spirit.

14. As it was in the begin<u>ning,</u> is now, *
    and will be forev<u>er</u>. Amen.

Psalm Three

[Tone 3]

[For special occasion, see p. 155.]

(Christ the Hero addresses the Father.)

1. Have mercy on me, O God, have <u>mer</u>cy, *
   for my soul trusts in <u>you</u>. *
2. Shadow me beneath your wings of <u>hope</u> *
   until iniquity pas<u>ses</u> by.

3. I will call to my Father most holy, most <u>high</u>, *
   to God my bene<u>fac</u>tor. *
4. God sent help from heaven and <u>freed</u> me, *
   God disgraced those <u>who</u> trampled me.

5. God sent mercy and truth; /
   God snatched my soul from my fiercest <u>en</u>emies, *
   from those who hated me, /
   who were confident a<u>gainst</u> me. *
6. They rigged a trap for my <u>feet</u> *
   and they buckled <u>my</u> soul.

7. They dug a <u>pit</u> for me *
   and into it they have <u>fal</u>len. *
8. I am prepared, O God, / my heart is <u>ready</u>, *
   I will sing and chant <u>a</u> psalm.

Psalm 3

9. Arise, my glory, / arise psaltery and <u>harp</u>, *
   I will arise at <u>dawn</u>. *
10. I will confess you before peoples, O <u>Lord</u>, *
    I will chant you a psalm a<u>mong</u> nations.

11. For your mercy has reached even to the <u>heavens</u>, *
    and even to the clouds, your <u>truth</u>. *
12. Be exalted above the heavens, O <u>God</u>, *
    and over all the earth be <u>your</u> glory.

13. Glory to the Father and to the <u>Son</u> *
    and to the Holy <u>Spi</u>rit. *
14. As it was in the beginning, is <u>now</u>, *
    and will be forever. <u>A</u>men.

Psalm Four

[Tone 1]

[For special occasion, see p. 155.]

(Christ the Hero addresses the Father.)

1. Have mercy on me, O God, /
   for all have trampled me un<u>der</u>foot; *
   they troubled me, / attack<u>ing</u> me all day long.

2. All day long my enemies have trampled me un<u>der</u>foot; *
   how numerous those who have waged <u>war</u> against me.

3. All my enemies were against me, /
   they were thinking evil things <u>of</u> me; *
   they spread a wicked <u>word</u> about me.

4. Those who were guarding <u>my</u> life *
   were schem<u>ing</u> against me.

5. They were going <u>out</u>side *
   and were plot<u>ting</u> together.

6. All who saw me laughed <u>at</u> me; *
   their lips spoke <u>and</u> their heads shook.

7. I am a worm, a <u>non</u>-human, *
   a human disgrace, / an outcast <u>of</u> the people.

Psalm 4

8. Far more than all my enemies, /
   I have become a total disgrace to <u>my</u> neighbors *
   and a dread to <u>my</u> acquaintances.

9. Holy Father, / keep not your aid far <u>from </u>me; *
   my God, / see to <u>my</u> assistance!

10. Make haste <u>to</u> help me, *
    Lord, God of <u>my</u> salvation!

11. Glory to the Father and to <u>the</u> Son *
    and to the <u>Ho</u>ly Spirit.

12. As it was in the beginning, <u>is</u> now, *
    and will be for<u>ev</u>er. Amen.

Psalm Five

[Tone 3]

[For special occasion, see p. 155.]

(Christ the Hero addresses Francis.)

1. With my voice I cried out to the <u>Lord</u>, *
   with my voice I pleaded with the <u>Lord</u>. *
2. In God's sight I poured out my <u>prayer</u>, *
   before God the story of <u>my</u> troubles.

3. My spirit was failing with<u>in</u> me, *
   but you, / you knew my <u>paths</u>. *
4. On this road I was <u>walk</u>ing *
   the arrogant have hidden a trap <u>for</u> me.

5. I looked to my right and <u>saw</u> *
   that no one recog<u>nized</u> me. *
6. There is no es<u>cape</u>; *
   no one cares for <u>my</u> life.

7. Because of you I have endured dis<u>grace</u>, *
   confusion has covered my <u>face</u>. *
8. I became a stranger to <u>my</u> kin, *
   and a pilgrim to my moth<u>er's</u> children.

(Christ the Hero addresses the Father.)

Psalm 5

9. Holy Father, / zeal for your house has con<u>sum</u>ed me, *
    and the abuses of your attackers have fallen on <u>me</u>. *
10. They rejoiced and united a<u>gainst</u> me; *
    they scourged me and I knew <u>not</u> why.

11. They outnumber the hairs of my <u>head</u>, *
    those who hate me without <u>cause</u>. *
12. My enemies have been <u>streng</u>thened, *
    those who persecuted me unjustly; /
    they made me repay what I did <u>not</u> steal.

13. Evil witnesses rose up, / questioned <u>me</u> *
    on things I knew nothing a<u>bout</u>. *
14. They were repaying me evil for <u>good</u>; *
    they were slandering me for pursu<u>ing</u> goodness.

15. You are my most holy <u>Fa</u>ther, *
    my king and my <u>God</u>. *
16. Make haste to <u>help</u> me, *
    Lord, God of my <u>sal</u>vation!

17. Glory to the Father and to the <u>Son</u> *
    and to the Holy <u>Spi</u>rit. *
18. As it was in the beginning, is <u>now</u>, *
    and will be forever. <u>A</u>men.

Psalm Six

[Tone 5]

[For special occasion, see p. 156.]

(Christ the Hero addresses the people.)

1. O you / who pass a<u>long</u> this way, *
   look and see if there is a sorrow <u>like</u> mine.

2. For a pack of dogs has sur<u>round</u>ed me *
   a gang of evildoers has closed in <u>on</u> me.

3. Yes, they have stared at me and gloated; /
   they have divided my <u>clothes</u> among them *
   and have cast lots for <u>my</u> tunic.

4. They have pierced my hands <u>and</u> my feet; *
   they have counted all <u>my</u> bones.

5. They have opened their <u>mouth</u> against me *
   like a ravening and roar<u>ing</u> lion.

6. I have been poured <u>out</u> like water *
   and all my bones have been pulled <u>a</u>part.

7. My heart has become like <u>melt</u>ing wax *
   within <u>my</u> being.

8. My strength has dried up <u>like</u> baked clay *
   my tongue has stuck to <u>my</u> palate

Psalm 6

9. They have given me poison <u>for</u> my food *
   and vinegar to slake <u>my</u> thirst.

10. They have led me into the <u>dust</u> of death; *
    they have added to the pain of <u>my</u> wounds.

11. I have slept / and <u>I</u> have risen, *
    and my most holy Father has received me <u>with</u> glory.

(Christ the Hero addresses the Father.)

12. Holy Father, you have held my right hand; /
    you have drawn me <u>by</u> your will *
    and have lifted me up <u>with</u> glory.

(Christ the Hero addresses the people.)

13. For what else is in heav<u>en</u> for me, *
    and besides you, / what have I wanted <u>on</u> earth?

14. Behold and see that I am God, says the Lord; /
    supreme a<u>mong</u> the nations, *
    supreme on <u>the</u> earth.

(Francis addresses the people.)

15. Blessed be the Lord, the God of Israel, /
    who has redeemed the souls of his servants /
    with his own most <u>ho</u>ly blood, *
    and who will not abandon those who hope in <u>the</u> Lord.

16. And we know that the <u>Lord</u> is coming, *
    and will come to <u>judge</u> justice.

17. Glory to the Father and <u>to</u> the Son *
    and to the Ho<u>ly</u> Spirit.

18. As it was in the begin<u>ning,</u> is now, *
    and will be forev<u>er</u>. Amen.

Psalm Seven

[Tone 4]

[For special occasion, see p. 155.]

(Francis addresses the people.)

1. Clap your hands, <u>all</u> you peoples; *
   raise to God a shout of exul<u>ta</u>tion and joy.

2. Because the Lord <u>is</u> the Most High, *
   the awesome, great King o<u>ver</u> all the earth.

3. For the most holy Father of heaven,
   our King before all ages, /
   sent the beloved Son <u>from</u> on high, *
   who planted salvation in the cen<u>ter</u> of the earth.

4. Let heavens rejoice and earth exult, /
   let the sea and all that is <u>in</u> it roar, *
   let fields and everything in <u>them</u> sing for joy.

5. Sing a new song <u>to</u> the Lord; *
   all the earth <u>sing</u> to the Lord!

6. For the Lord is great and worthy <u>of</u> high praise; *
   worthy of awe <u>a</u>bove all gods.

7. Bring to the Lord, families of nations, /
   bring to the Lord glo<u>ry</u> and honor; *
   bring to the Lord the glo<u>ry</u> due his name.

Psalm 7

8. Cast off the weight of sin /
   and take up the Lord's <u>ho</u>ly cross; *
   and follow the Lord's most holy commands
   to <u>the</u> very end.

During Advent this psalm ends here.

9. Let the whole earth delight before <u>the</u> Lord's face; *
   say among nations: /
   the Lord has reigned from the <u>wood</u> of a cross.

From Ascension to the beginning of Advent the following verses are added:

10. And the Lord ascended <u>in</u>to heaven *
    and is seated at the right hand of the most holy <u>Father</u>
    in heaven.

11. Be exalted above the heav<u>ens</u>, O God; *
    above all the <u>earth</u> be your glory.

12. And we know that the <u>Lord</u> is coming *
    and will <u>come</u> to judge justice.

13. Glory to the Father and <u>to</u> the Son *
    and to <u>the</u> Holy Spirit.

14. As it was in the begin<u>ning,</u> is now, *
    and will be for<u>ev</u>er. Amen.

Psalm Eight

[Tone 5]

[For special occasion, see p. 156.]

(Christ the Hero addresses the Father.)

1. God, see to <u>my</u> assistance; *
   Lord, hasten <u>to</u> help me.

2. May they be confound<u>ed</u> and shamed, *
   those who covet <u>my</u> soul.

3. May they be repelled and <u>blush</u> with shame, *
   those who wish <u>me</u> evil.

4. May they retreat at <u>once</u> in shame *
   those who jeer at me: / Well done! <u>Well</u> done!

5. But <u>they</u> who seek you, *
   may they exult and rejoice <u>in</u> you,

6. And may lovers of your salva<u>tion</u> repeat: *
   May the Lord be mag<u>ni</u>fied!

7. But as for me, / I am nee<u>dy</u> and poor; *
   O <u>God</u>, help me.

8. You are my helper, my <u>lib</u>erator, *
   Lord, do not <u>de</u>lay.

Psalm 8

9. Glory to the Father and <u>to</u> the Son *
   and to the Ho<u>ly</u> Spirit.

10. As it was in the begin<u>ning,</u> is now, *
    and will be forever. <u>A</u>men.

Psalm Nine

[Tone 3]

[For special occasion, see p. 155.]

(Francis addresses the crowd.)

1. Sing a new song to the <u>Lord</u>, *
   the worker of wondrous <u>deeds</u>. *
2. God's right hand and <u>ho</u>ly arm *
   sacrificed the belov<u>ed</u> Son.

3. The Lord made salvation <u>known</u>, *
   revealed justice to the <u>na</u>tions. *
4. On that day the Lord sent <u>mer</u>cy *
   and song in <u>the</u> night.

5. This is the day the <u>Lord</u> has made; *
   let us rejoice and be <u>glad</u> in it. *
6. Blessed is the one who comes in the name of the <u>Lord</u>; *
   the Lord is God, and has shone <u>up</u>on us.

7. Let the heavens rejoice and earth exult, /
   let the sea and all that is in it <u>roar</u>, *
   let the fields and everything in them sing for <u>joy</u>. *
8. Bring to the Lord, families of nations, /
   bring to the Lord glory and <u>hon</u>or, *
   bring to the Lord the glory due <u>his</u> name.

Psalm 9

The following four verses are added:
- *on weekdays from the Ascension to the Octave of Pentecost;*
- *on Sundays and major feastdays from Ascension to Advent and from the Octave of Epiphany to Holy Thursday.*

9. Kingdoms of the earth sing to <u>God</u>, *
   chant psalms to the <u>Lord</u>. *
10. Chant psalms to the One who ascended to the <u>East</u> *
    above the heaven <u>of</u> heavens.
11. Behold, / God speaks with a voice of <u>power</u>; *
    give glory to God, who governs Israel, /
    whose splendor and power is on <u>high</u>. *
12. God, wonderful in the saints, / the very God of <u>Israel</u>, *
    will give the people power and might. / Blessed <u>be</u> God!
13. Glory to the Father and to the <u>Son</u> *
    and to the Holy <u>Spirit</u>. *
14. As it was in the beginning, is <u>now</u>, *
    and will be forever. <u>A</u>men.

Psalm Ten

[Tone 4]

[For special occasion, see p. 155.]

(Francis to the people—to the whole earth.)

1. All the earth, shout joyfully to the Lord, /
   chant a psalm <u>to</u> God's name; *
   glori<u>fy</u> God with praise.

2. Say to God: / "How awesome are your <u>deeds</u>, O Lord; *
   confronted with your mighty strength /
   your enemies shall recognize they <u>have</u> lied about you.

3. May all the earth adore you / and sing <u>psalms</u> to you; *
   may it chant a <u>psalm</u> to your name."

(Christ the hero addresses the people.)

4. Come, listen, all you <u>who</u> fear God, *
   and I will recount how much God has <u>done</u>
   for my soul.

5. I cried out to God <u>with</u> my mouth, *
   high <u>praise</u> on my tongue.

6. And from the holy temple God <u>heard</u> my voice, *
   my crying <u>out</u> in God's sight.

Psalm 10

(Francis to the people—to the whole earth.)

7. Bless our <u>God</u>, you peoples, *
   voice the <u>sound</u> of God's praise.

8. Every race on earth shall be <u>blessed</u> in God, *
   and all nations shall <u>mag</u>nify God.

9. Blessed be the Lord, the <u>God</u> of Israel *
   who <u>a</u>lone works wonders.

10. And blessed forever be God's <u>glo</u>rious name, *
    may the whole earth be filled with God's glory. /
    <u>A</u>men! Amen!

11. Glory to the Father and <u>to</u> the Son *
    and to <u>the</u> Holy Spirit.

12. As it was in the begin<u>ning</u>, is now, *
    and will be for<u>ev</u>er. Amen.

Psalm Eleven

[Tone 2]

[For special occasion, see p. 155.]

(Francis addresses the Hero and then the people [6b, 7a, 8–9].)

1. May the Lord hear you in <u>time</u> of trouble; *
   may the name of the God of Ja<u>cob</u> protect you.

2. May God send you help from the <u>ho</u>ly place, *
   and may God care for <u>you</u> from Zion.

3. May God be mindful of <u>all</u> your sacrifice, *
   and may your burnt offerings <u>be</u> agreeable.

4. May God grant you your <u>heart's</u> desire, *
   and fulfill your <u>ev</u>ery plan.

5. We will rejoice <u>in</u> your victory, *
   and in the name of our God we will be <u>lift</u>ed up.

6. May the Lord grant all <u>your</u> requests. *
   Now I have known that the Lord God sent the Son, Jesus Christ, /
   who will judge the peo<u>ples</u> with justice.

Psalm 11

7. And the Lord has become a refuge for the <u>poor</u>, /
   a helper in <u>times</u> of trouble; *
   and may they, who have come to know your name,
   <u>hope</u> in you.

8. Blessed be the <u>Lord</u> my God, *
   who has become my protector and refuge in my <u>day</u> of
   trouble.

9. O my helper, I will <u>sing</u> to you, *
   for you, O God, are my protector, /
   my <u>God</u>, my mercy!

10. Glory to the Father and <u>to</u> the Son *
    and to the <u>Ho</u>ly Spirit.

11. As it was in the begin<u>ning</u>, is now, *
    and will be forev<u>er</u>. Amen.

Psalm Twelve

[Tone 5]

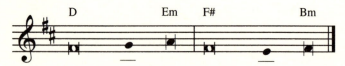

[For special occasion, see p. 156.]

(Christ the Hero addresses the Father.)

1. In you, O Lord, I have hoped /
   let me not be <u>shamed</u> forever; *
   in your justice deliver me, / res<u>cue</u> me.

2. Be attentive <u>to</u> my call, *
   and <u>save</u> me.

3. Be for me a protector-God <u>and</u> a fortress, *
   keep <u>me</u> safe.

4. For you are my pa<u>tience</u>, O Lord,*
   my hope since <u>my</u> childhood.

5. In you I have been strengthened from the womb, /
   from my birth you are <u>my</u> protector; *
   you will always be <u>my</u> song.

6. May my mouth be filled with praise /
   that I may <u>sing</u> your glory, *
   your greatness all <u>day</u> long.

7. Answer me, O Lord, / for kind <u>is</u> your mercy; *
   with the multitude of your mer<u>cies</u> turn to me.

Psalm 12

8. And turn not your face <u>from</u> your child; *
   answer me quickly for I am <u>in</u> anguish.

9. Blessed be the Lord my God, /
   who has become my protec<u>tor</u> and refuge *
   in my day <u>of</u> trouble.

10. O my helper, I will sing to you, /
    for you, O God are <u>my</u> protector, *
    my God, <u>my</u> mercy!

11. Glory to the Father and <u>to</u> the Son *
    and to the Ho<u>ly</u> Spirit.

12. As it was in the begin<u>ning,</u> is now, *
    and will be forever. <u>A</u>men.

Psalm Thirteen

[Tone 1]

[For special occasion, see p. 155.]

(Christ the Hero addresses the Father.)

1. How long, O Lord, in the end will you <u>forget</u> me? *
   How long will you turn your <u>face</u> from me?

2. How long shall I bear conflict in <u>my</u> soul, *
   pain in my heart all <u>through</u> the day?

3. How long will my enemy be victorious o<u>ver</u> me? *
   Look at me and hear me, / O <u>Lord</u>, my God.

4. Enlighten my eyes that I may not fall
   into <u>death's</u> sleep,*
   that my enemy may never say: / "I <u>have</u> prevailed."

5. Those who torment me would rejoice
   if I be<u>came</u> troubled; *
   but I hoped <u>in</u> your mercy.

6. My heart shall delight in <u>your</u> victory; *
   I will sing to the Lord who granted good things to me, /
   and I will sing to the name of the <u>Lord</u>, Most High.

Psalm 13

7. Glory to the Father and to the Son *
   and to the Holy Spirit.

8. As it was in the beginning, is now, *
   and will be forever. Amen.

Psalm Fourteen

[Tone 4]

[For special occasion, see p. 155.]

(Christ the Hero addresses the Father.)

1. I will confess you, Lord, most holy Father, /
   King of heav<u>en</u> and earth, *
   for <u>you</u> have consoled me.

2. You are <u>God</u>, my Savior; *
   I will act confidently and <u>not</u> be afraid.

3. You, O Lord, are my strength <u>and</u> my praise, *
   you have be<u>come</u> my salvation.

4. Your right hand, O Lord, is magnificent strength, /
   your right hand, O Lord, has <u>struck</u> the enemy; *
   and in your great glory you <u>de</u>posed my adversaries.

(Francis addresses the people.)

5. Let the poor see <u>and</u> rejoice; *
   seek the Lord and <u>your</u> soul will live.

6. For the Lord <u>heard</u> the poor, *
   and has <u>not</u> scorned those captive.

7. Let heaven and <u>earth</u> praise God, *
   the seas and all <u>that</u> moves in them.

Psalm 14

8. For God will secure Zion, *
   and the cities of Judah will be rebuilt.

9. And the poor will dwell there, *
   and will inherit Zion.

10. And the descendants of God's servants will possess it *
    and those who love God's name will live in it.

11. Glory to the Father and to the Son *
    and to the Holy Spirit.

12. As it was in the beginning, is now, *
    and will be forever. Amen.

Psalm Fifteen

[Tone 4]

[For special occasion, see p. 155.]

(Francis addresses the people.)

1. Sing for joy to <u>God</u> our help; *
   with exultant voice /
   raise to the Lord God living and true <u>a</u> shout of joy.

2. Because the Lord <u>is</u> the Most High, *
   the awesome, great King o<u>ver</u> all the earth.

3. For the most holy Father of heaven, /
   our King be<u>fore</u> all ages, *
   sent from on high the beloved Son /
   who was born of the Blessed Vir<u>gin</u>, Holy Mary.

4. He called out to God: / You <u>are</u> my Father, *
   and God placed him as the firstborn, /
   the highest above <u>all</u> earthly kings.

5. On that day the <u>Lord</u> sent mercy *
   and <u>song</u> in the night.

6. This is the day the <u>Lord</u> has made; *
   let us rejoice in <u>it</u> and be glad.

Psalm 15

7. For to us is given the beloved child most holy, /
   born for us along the way and placed <u>in</u> a manger *
   because there was no room for <u>him</u> at the inn.

8. Glory to the Lord God <u>in</u> the highest *
   and on earth peace to <u>those</u> of good will.

9. Let heavens rejoice and earth exult, /
   let the sea and all that is <u>in</u> it roar, *
   let fields and everything in <u>them</u> sing for joy

10. Sing to the <u>Lord</u> a new song; *
    sing to the <u>Lord</u>, all the earth!

11. For the Lord is great and highly <u>to</u> be praised; *
    more awe<u>some</u> than all gods.

12. Bring to the Lord, families of nations, /
    bring to the Lord glo<u>ry</u> and honor, *
    bring to the Lord the glo<u>ry</u> due his name.

13. Cast off the weight of sin /
    and take up the Lord's <u>ho</u>ly cross, *
    follow the Lord's most holy commands to <u>the</u> very end.

14. Glory to the Father and <u>to</u> the Son *
    and to <u>the</u> Holy Spirit.

15. As it was in the begin<u>ning</u>, is now, *
    and will be for<u>ev</u>er. Amen.

[Since this psalm is used constantly during the Christmas Season, a second tone is provided for variety.]

Psalm Fifteen

[Tone 2]

[For special occasion, see p. 155.]

(Francis addresses the people.)

1. Sing for joy to <u>God</u> our help; *
   with exultant voice /
   raise to the Lord God living and true a <u>shout</u> of joy.

2. Because the Lord <u>is</u> the Most High, *
   the awesome, great King over <u>all</u> the earth.

3. For the most holy Father of heav<u>en</u>, /
   our King be<u>fore</u> all ages, *
   sent from on high the beloved Son /
   who was born of the Blessed Virgin, <u>Ho</u>ly Mary.

4. He called out to <u>God</u>: / You <u>are</u> my Father, *
   and God placed him as the firstborn, /
   the highest above all <u>earth</u>ly kings.

5. On that day the <u>Lord</u> sent mercy *
   and song <u>in</u> the night.

6. This is the day the <u>Lord</u> has made; *
   let us rejoice in it <u>and</u> be glad.

Psalm 15

7. For to us is given the beloved child most ho<u>ly</u>, /
   born for us along the way and placed <u>in</u> a manger *
   because there was no room for him <u>at</u> the inn.

8. Glory to the Lord God <u>in</u> the highest *
   and on earth peace to those <u>of</u> good will.

9. Let heavens rejoice and earth ex<u>ult</u>, /
   let the sea and all that is <u>in</u> it roar, *
   let fields and everything in them <u>sing</u> for joy

10. Sing to the Lord <u>a</u> new song; *
    sing to the Lord, <u>all</u> the earth!

11. For the Lord is great and highly <u>to</u> be praised; *
    more awesome <u>than</u> all gods.

12. Bring to the Lord, families of na<u>tions</u>, /
    bring to the Lord glo<u>ry</u> and honor, *
    bring to the Lord the glory <u>due</u> his name.

13. Cast off the weight of <u>sin</u> /
    and take up the Lord's <u>holy</u> cross, *
    follow the Lord's most holy commands to the <u>very</u> end.

14. Glory to the Father and <u>to</u> the Son *
    and to the <u>Holy</u> Spirit.

15. As it was in the begin<u>ning</u>, is now, *
    and will be forev<u>er</u>. Amen.

Blessing–Dismissal

Without instrument

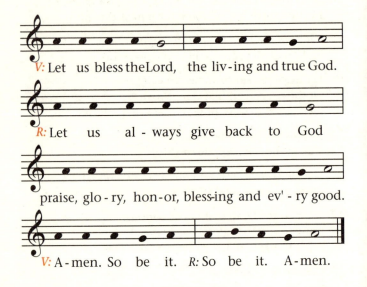

V: Let us bless the Lord, the liv-ing and true God.

R: Let us al-ways give back to God praise, glo-ry, hon-or, bless-ing and ev'-ry good.

V: A-men. So be it. R: So be it. A-men.

For piano, organ or guitar

For 3 voices

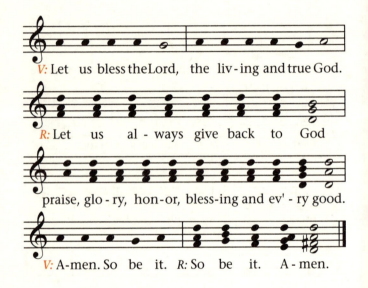

SECTION TWO

COMMENTARY

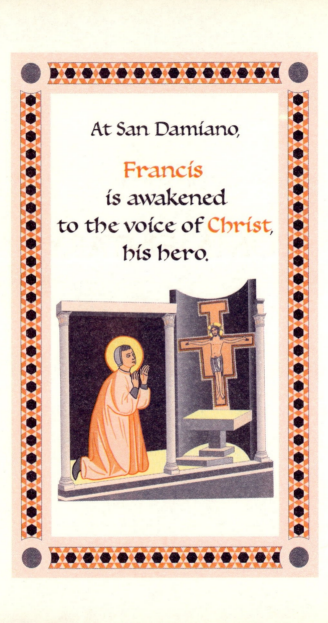

Introduction

The Existing Collection

Francis of Assisi's writings, though not very numerous nor lengthy, nevertheless contain many gems. The best known is surely the *Canticle of Brother Sun*. The least known, but without doubt the most original, is the collection of liturgically-inspired texts which comprise his *Office of the Passion*. Over the centuries these texts were either ignored or at best considered an interesting but not very significant collection of scriptural quotations. And it was only after Paul Sabatier, the initiator of modern Franciscan studies, called attention to this Little Office at the beginning of the 20th century, did its status slowly emerge as an authentic spiritual gem.

Francis *Office of the Passion* includes:
- a hymn;
- a prayer;
- an antiphon;
- 15 "psalms";
- a blessing-dismissal.

In the manuscripts of this Little Office scribes have added descriptive texts and rubrics which explain how Francis organized and prayed these texts.

Commentary

The Origin of This Collection of Texts

Votive or devotional offices were common in Francis' day. Two models existed. A longer model followed the structure of the Liturgy of Hours, while a shorter model usually consisted of only three components: a hymn, a short reading or antiphon, and a prayer. Francis' Little Office occupies a middle position between these two clearly defined traditional forms because Francis' office was not initially planned as a votive office. In fact, what evidence can be gathered indicates that it was not composed according to a predetermined plan, but first existed only as a variety of separate elements which gradually came together to create this unique form of prayer.

Francis' Little Office evolved over many years from about the time of his conversion until his death, as much in its general form as in the content of its various components. This evolution is not easy to reconstruct, but some significant factors can be identified:

• Francis placed the *Prayer* immediately after the opening *Praises* rather than at the end of the office.

• From very early on, Francis' was accustomed to the practice of amplifying existing liturgical texts to give voice to his prayer and that of the fraternity. Verse 5 of the *Testament* where he takes an antiphon from the feast of the Exaltation of the Cross and adapts it ("We adore you, Lord Jesus Christ. . ."), is a good example of this.

Introduction

- Some psalms are practically taken as they appear in the psalter, whereas others represent highly complex composites drawn from many sources.

Concerning the history of this Little Office, these factors, together with clues found occasionally in the texts themselves, lead to the hypothesis that the office could have evolved from three components, quite different from one another:

1. a "commemoration";
2. a Nativity "song";
3. a series of five psalms prayed in honor of the Five Wounds of Christ.

Because of Francis' great devotion to Mary, the Mother of Christ, one could possibly add another independent component: an invocation to the Virgin.

1. A Commemoration

A "commemoration" was a short liturgical prayer composed of:

- a biblical or biblically inspired text in the manner of an antiphon;
- a versicle and a response;
- a prayer.

One or more of these commemorations were routinely added to the Liturgy of Hours whether for special devotions, for saints or for the deceased. Francis' commemoration focused on the glorification of God and possibly of the Lamb, and would have consisted of the following material:

Commentary

- as the antiphon, one or all of the quotations from the book of Revelation now found in the three first verses of the *Praises*;
- a versicle followed by the response: Let us praise...;
- the prayer with more or less the same content as the one that now accompanies the *Praises*.

The antiphon (1) could have very well represented an evolution of an older practice where Francis would simply have repeated the acclamation which concludes the preface of the eucharistic prayer: "Holy, holy, holy, Lord God of power and might. . . . " The triple repetition, "Holy, holy, holy," would have suggested to Francis the replacement of the eucharistic acclamation with that of the timeless celestial liturgy as described in chapters 4 and 5 of the book of Revelation: **Holy, Holy, Holy Lord God Almighty, Who is and Who was and Who is to come** [4:8]. The versicle (2) could have corresponded either to the present verses 4 or 5 of the *Praises*. Verse 4 would have emphasized the Trinitarian focus of the praise (**Let us bless the Father and the Son and the Holy Spirit**); and verse 5, its cosmic dimension (**All you works of the Lord, bless the Lord**).

Because of the praise content of Francis' commemoration, one can envision that it was rapidly moved to the beginning of the Liturgy of Hours where it then served as an introduction. In this new position, it evolved toward its present form of a hymn or praise. The second half of the *Praises* [vs. 5–8]—the invitation to all of creation to join in the celestial praise—has a forerunner in Francis' *Exhortation to the Praise of God*. The prayer (3), which echoes the same praise objective, was kept together with the *Praises* as its complement.

INTRODUCTION

2. A Nativity Song

A comparative study of PsF 7, 9 and 15 show that they evolved from what we can identify as a previous "Nativity Song" composed by Francis which was composed of some of the common material one finds in these three psalms of Francis:

- the mention of **his beloved Son**;
- the invitation to **let heavens rejoice . . . earth exult . . . the sea be moved . . . the field . . . be glad**;
- the call to **bring to the Lord families of nations . . . glory and honor . . . the glory due his name**.

3. Psalms in Honor of the Five Wounds

From the 11th century onward, we find evidence of devotion to the Five Wounds of Jesus. The common practice would be to repeat a formula such as the Our Father for each of the wounds. And we know from the *Legend of St. Clare* [30] that she prayed not only the "Office of the Cross" which Francis composed, but also a series of prayers in honor of the Five Wounds. (The prayers sometimes alluded to as Clare's prayers to the Five Wounds are of a later date.)

From the texts now found in the *Office of the Passion*, one can conclude that Francis would have chosen a different biblical psalm for each of the Five Wounds. Over time, these psalms evolved towards a formal "song" structure (2 groups of 4 verses), where material from other psalms gradually substituted for certain verses of the originally chosen psalms, so as to evoke more vividly five scenes of the Passion:

COMMENTARY

- the arrest in Gethsemani;
- the encounter with the Sanhedrin;
- the trial before Pilate;
- the agony and suffering;
- the death on the Cross.

The Evolution Towards a Little Office

Inspired by the ancient custom of praying the Liturgy of Hours in conjunction with an episode of the Passion of Christ, the five "Passion Songs" were then linked to the Hours more closely associated with the events they evoked:

1. Compline (before retiring for the night)
   – the arrest in Gethsemani;
2. Matins-Lauds (in the middle of the night)
   – the encounter with the Sanhedrin;
3. Terce (at nine in the morning)
   – the trial before Pilate;
4. Sext (at noon)
   – the agony and suffering;
5. None (at three in the afternoon)
   – the death on the Cross.

For the two remaining Hours, Francis chose two biblical psalms: 56 for Prime (before the beginning of the day's work) and 29 for Vespers (at sunset). Psalm 29 was later replaced by PsF 7, an offshoot of the original Nativity song.

The aforementioned Passion songs and the *Praises* were gradually rearranged in the form of the *Office of the Passion* as we know it today. In this evolution, an antiphon, possibly based on an earlier invocation to Mary, and a blessing-dismissal were added to echo the praise orientation of the *Praises* and prayer. And while the content of Francis' compositions noted above continued to evolve, he chose other biblical psalms and gradually reworked them to replace the initial series during other liturgical seasons: Easter, Sundays and Feastdays, Advent, Christmas.

One should not imagine Francis composing his Little Office sitting at a desk with parchment and quill in hand. According to the custom of his time, it was primarily by means of the psalter that Francis would have learned to read. Moreover, he daily prayed the Liturgy of the Hours, of which the psalms constitute a major part. And as St. Bonaventure points out, his remarkable memory would retain what he would read in Scripture and on which he would continually meditate [LMj 10:1]. It was during the very act of praying these texts that Francis would modify, add to or substitute psalm verses according to the movement of his contemplation.

Assigning dates to the various stages of Francis' Little Office is practically impossible. However, on the basis of the general context, one can surmise that the whole process would have begun around 1215 and evolved over a period of some ten to twelve years. So what is now known as Francis' votive office is the result of the gradual transformation of the various elements mentioned above, as they stood at the time of Francis' death in 1226. Had he lived longer, his Little Office would most likely have continued evolving so as to reflect more closely Francis' ever-deepening contemplative grasp of the Christ mystery.

An Introduction to A Christian Reading of The Psalms

Francis' liturgical treatment of the psalms is rooted in the foundational writings of Christianity. From the beginning, the New Testament writings apply verses of the psalms to Christ. Later on, as the psalms were being more commonly used in the early Church's liturgy, especially from the fourth century when the book of Psalms was adopted as the basis of monastic prayer life, Christians sought to interpret the whole psalter in the light of the mystery of Christ. One finds many examples of this in the sermons and commentaries of the Fathers of the Church. Shortly afterwards there appear short introductory titles given each psalm or rubrics such as "Christ to the Father," "The Church to Christ," which link the psalms to Christ. Finally, prayers were composed and added as conclusions to the psalms. Through these prayers various aspects of the Christian mystery were linked to expressions or images found in the psalms.

We also find collections of psalm verses gathered under various headings such as thanksgiving, supplication, confession of sins.

Francis takes this process one step further. His "psalms" are indeed collections of psalm verses; however, they are constructed from carefully selected material so as to express a clearly identified intention which is to evoke the geste of Christ, his Hero, and its cosmic consequences not only for our lives but also for the fate of the whole universe.

Introduction

Francis prepared himself to celebrate each canonical hour by praying one of his psalms. In so doing he entered into a Christian reading of the psalms which comprised the bulk of the canonical office which followed.

A Quatrain Structure

When Francis sang of his Hero, he not only chose and masterfully crafted the building-blocks of his compositions, he also saw to their formal disposition. In fact, the number of verses that make up many of his psalms are multiples of 4: 8, 12, or 16 verses. Further observation reveals that the psalms of his Little Office can be broken down into sections generally made up of 4 verses. Since the four-verse unit, the quatrain, is a staple structure in poetry, it is possible to conclude that this quatrain form was Francis' basic reference for the structure of his psalms.

It must be added, though, that whereas the quatrain is made up of four usually rather short lines of text, the verses of biblical psalms, because of their length, often make up at least two lines of printed text. So while one can use the word "quatrain" in speaking of a group of four psalmic verses, it must be kept in mind that the term is here used in a broader sense than when applied to poetry.

Furthermore, it is clear that Francis did not consider himself a prisoner of the four-verse structure. As he reworked his texts to bring them into focus with his ever-deepening intuitions into the mystery of Christ, his Hero, he abandoned—apparently without regrets—the quatrain structure which had guided his first version of these texts. This is especially apparent in the psalms which make up the Hero's geste [PssF 1–6]. Because Francis prayed them frequently, he thus had more opportunity for reworking them. In the case of a few psalms of Francis, as will be pointed out in the individual commentaries, the quatrain structure is not found for the simple reason that, at the time of Francis' death, these psalms were still in an initial stage of composition.

In Search of A Name

Is the title *Office of the Passion* really appropriate for Francis Little Office? There is no information how Francis himself called his Little Office. The earliest known copies of Francis' writings simply identify the *Praises To Be Said at All the Hours* and "the psalms which the Blessed Francis put in order," inserting the *Antiphon* and *Blessing-dismissal* between PsF 1 and 2. In these same documents, it is only the first series [PsF 1–7] which is identified as the "psalms of the Passion."

The first to give it a specific name in the 13th century is Thomas of Celano in his life of St. Clare where, in paragraph 30, he speaks of "the office of the Cross." And it was in the 17th century that Luke Wadding, OFM, gave the ensemble of prayers the title *Office of the Passion*. Since then, this name has been used to designate the Little Office.

Introduction

In more recent times, various other titles have been proposed, such as "The Office of the Paschal Mystery." However, even though the Passion events inspire the main theme of his Little Office (PsF 1–6), Francis also evokes the birth, resurrection, glorification and second coming of his Hero. Therefore, it may be more appropriate to name it "The Office of the Mysteries of Christ."

Remarks on The Translations of Scriptural Texts Used in This Work

The Latin text of the Scriptures which Francis knew differed in many instances from today's translations which are based on a better knowledge of the Hebrew and Greek originals. These differences will prove important for Francis' *Office of the Passion*. For example, the Latin text which Francis uses in PsF 1:1a to set the scene of the Hero giving an account of his mission translates as follows:

> **O God, *I have given* you an account of my life . . . [Ps 55:8b–9]**.

Francis could not have introduced his Hero giving an account of his mission had he been composing from our modern translation of the same verse, whose subject pronoun (*I/You*) is different:

> "*You have kept* an account of my wanderings. . . ."

Also, today's translation of Ps 35:11

> "Lying witnesses *arise* and *accuse* me unjustly"

could not have been called upon to recount past events, as it does in PsF 5:13:

> **Evil witnesses standing up *were interrogating* me on what I knew nothing about.**

So as to remain within the scriptural context from which Francis' *Office of the Passion* emerged, all translations of the scriptural texts given in this work take into account the Latin texts of Francis' time. However, the numbers identifying psalms and verses follow the more recent standard English editions.

Latin Insertions

For the benefit of those readers who have some knowledge of Latin, the original language of Francis' Little Office, a few significant Latin words and expressions are inserted in the commentaries. However, always placed in parenthesis, these insertions are not part of the structure of the text and, therefore, do not affect its meaning. They are only meant to highlight the way Francis makes use of these words and expressions.

Also, to help the reader remember Francis' biblical choices, all citations from his Little Office in these commentaries—verses, expressions, individual words—are printed in **bold format**.

INTRODUCTION

About The Commentaries

Each component text of Francis' Little Office could warrant a rather lengthy commentary which would analyze his source material, his method of processing and harmonizing this material, and the relationship between the material he chooses and his personal experience reflected in his other writings. For the purpose of this work a choice has been made which integrates examples of the different aspects mentioned above, in the hope that the elements presented will help the reader eavesdrop, as it were, on Francis as he crafts these prayer texts. This could then become something of a window on Francis' prayer life and contemplation of Christ, his Hero, and consequently his vision of God's plan for creation. By frequently, or at least occasionally, experiencing Francis' approach to the mystery of Christ, his Hero-Teacher, one can enter more completely into the cosmic fullness of his gospel lifestyle.

Ordinary Components of the Office

Francis repeated some components of this Little Office at every Hour, namely:

- *Praises to Be Said at All the Hours* with its concluding *Prayer*
- *Antiphon*
- *Blessing-Dismissal*

Imagining
the ecstatic
symphony
surrounding the
heavenly throne,

Francis invites
all of creation
to join in the
praise of God
with one
cosmic voice!

COMMENTARY

Praises to Be Said at All the Hours

Introduction

The *Praises to Be Said at All the Hours* (hereafter abbreviated as *Praises)* provide, in the form of a hymn, the setting or the viewpoint from which Francis' geste of the great King is presented. It is worth noting that Francis first contemplates the Hero in his victory. In fact, the text of the hymn is constructed on the basis of the great celestial liturgy described by John in the book of Revelation, chapters 4 and 5, in which the four Living Beings, twenty-four Elders, and countless throngs of Angels surround and acclaim the Throne and the Lamb. Francis chooses for the first section of his hymn the acclamations of these three groups of worshipers.

One can assume that here Francis takes his cue for this hymn from the iconography of the churches of Rome, where the emphasis is precisely on the Lamb of God because "The Father abides in inaccessible light. . .and no one has ever seen God," as Francis recalls in his first *Admonition*, verse 5. The emphasis is, therefore, put on the One who reveals God. In fact, these scenes have been called the "adorations of the Lamb." The illustration reproduced herein demonstrates this by having Christ, in his human form and as the Lamb of God, occupy the central axis of the whole ensemble, as found in the church of St. Praxedes in Rome:

- on the triumphal arch, we see Christ between two angels in the center of the heavenly Jerusalem;

- at the top of the apse, the Lamb on his throne;
- then, the large figure of Christ advancing on the clouds;
- and finally, the Lamb on his mountain, from which flows the four rivers of life and towards which two processions of lambs advance from either side.

Furthermore, from the time of St. Irenaeus a traditional interpretation of the texts from Revelation quoted by Francis in the first three verses of the *Praises* has recognized the Incarnate Word in the Anonymous One seated on the throne. This interpretation draws upon what Jesus said to Philip in Jn 14:6–9: "Whoever has seen me has seen the Father." In fact, Francis opens his first *Admonition* with this very text.

In the *Praises*, it is in verse 3 that it becomes clear that the figure of the Lamb is the One to Whom the *Praises* are directed. Here also the Hero, who was slain, is now being acclaimed in his glory.

Commentary

In Rev 4–5 John describes the vision he had of the celestial liturgy. Caught up in the Spirit, he saw a door open in heaven:

> Behold a seat was placed in heaven and One seated on it. And the One who was sitting was similar in appearance to jasper and carnelian stone. . . . And around the seat there were . . . twenty-four elders . . . and four living creatures full of eyes in front and

behind. . . . And [the living creatures] had no rest day and night, saying: Holy, holy . . . [Rev 4:2–8].

Their acclamation opens Francis' *Praises*:

1. **Holy, Holy, Holy Lord God Almighty,
   Who is and Who was and Who is to come:** [cf. Rev 4:8]
   Let us praise and exalt him above all forever!

John's vision continues:

And as these living creatures gave glory and honor and blessing to the One seated on the throne . . . , the twenty-four elders came before the One seated on the throne and adored the One who lives forever and ever. And they cast their crowns before the throne saying: You are worthy, O Lord, our God, to receive praise and glory and honor and power, for you created all things and through your will . . . they were created [Rev 4:9–11].

For the second verse of his *Praises* Francis kept the beginning of the Elders' acclamation, but with a variant. He substituted **blessing** for the word "power":

2. **You are worthy, O Lord our God,
   to receive praise and glory and honor
   and blessing:** [cf. Rev 4:11]
   Let us praise and exalt him above all forever!

Then in John's vision two new actors, the Lamb and the choir of Angels, appear:

Praises to Be Said at All the Hours

And in the right hand of the One seated on the throne, I saw a book written inside and out. . . . And behold between the throne and the four living creatures and the elders [was] an apparently slain Lamb. . . . And he came and accepted the book from the right hand of the One seated on the throne. . . . And I heard the voice of numerous angels around the throne, the living creatures and the elders; and their number was thousands of thousands, saying in a loud voice: Worthy is the Lamb . . . [Rev 5:1–12].

And their acclamation becomes verse 3 of Francis' *Praises:*

3. **Worthy is the Lamb who was slain
      to receive power and divinity and wisdom
      and strength and honor
      and glory and blessing: [Rev 5:12]
   Let us praise and exalt him above all
      forever!**

By referring to John's vision in the first three verses cited above, Francis conjures up in his mind, as it were, a "spiritual cathedral" in which resounds an unending symphony of celestial praise. In verse 4, Francis makes it clear that this praise, addressed to and focused upon the victorious Lamb, opens up to include the entire Trinity:

4. **Let us bless the Father and the Son and
      the Holy Spirit:
   Let us praise and exalt him above all
      forever!**

COMMENTARY

Francis appropriates the Trinitarian theme of his verse 4 from the Sunday morning Liturgy of the Hours, and in so doing, he discovers there the refrain he uses throughout his entire hymn: **Let us praise and exalt him above all forever!** In this refrain Francis not only invites creation to praise and exalt, but to "super-exalt" *(superexaltemus)*, to exalt the Triune God in the highest degree possible.

*

Immersed in this praise, Francis feels motivated to invite all of creation, including himself, to join in this unending symphony. This he does in the following verse which he found in the same Sunday morning liturgical text:

> 5. **All you works of the Lord, bless the Lord:**
>   [Dan 3:57]
>   **Let us praise and exalt him above all forever!**

After this general call to all of creation, Francis enumerates the various categories of beings that he invites to this praise. Having already mentioned the celestial beings in the first verses of his *Praises*, he calls upon humanity. And for this he reverts to John's book of Revelation, chapter 19:

> I heard the voice of a great crowd in heaven, saying: "Alleluia! Salvation and glory and power belong to our God. . . ." And the twenty-four elders and the four living creatures fell down and adored God seated on the throne saying: "Amen! Alleluia!" And from

the throne a voice came saying: **Give praise to our God, all you his servants and you who fear God, the small and the great.** And I heard the voice of a vast crowd, like the voice of great waters, and like the voice of loud thunder saying: "Alleluia! For the Lord our Almighty God reigns. Let us rejoice and exult and give him glory . . . " [Rev 19:1, 4–7].

This scene was exactly what Francis needed to call humanity to join in the heavenly choirs:

6. **Give praise to our God, all you his servants and you who fear God,
   the small and the great:** [Rev 19:5]
   Let us praise and exalt him above all forever!

Rev 5:12 had supplied Francis with the acclamation of verse 3 of his *Praises*. The following verse [Rev 5:13] sets the tone and supplies the material Francis needed for his next verses to continue his invitation to all of creation:

And every creature that is in heaven and on the earth and under the earth and those who are in the sea. . . . I heard them all saying: "To the One sitting on the throne and to the Lamb, blessing and honor. . . ."

By combining Rev 5:13 with material taken from Ps 68:35, Francis, in verses 7 and 8, then calls upon the heavens, the earth and the sea, and all the creatures that populate them, to add their voices to what truly becomes a cosmic symphony of praise:

COMMENTARY

7. **Let heaven and earth praise that glorious One:** [cf Ps 68:35a]
   Let us praise and exalt him above all forever!

8. **And every creature that is in heaven and on the earth and under the earth,** [Rev 5:13]
   and the sea and all that is in it: [Ps 68:35b]
   Let us praise and exalt him above all forever!

*

The concluding doxology underlines once again the Trinitarian dimension of Christian prayer:

9. **Glory to the Father and to the Son and to the Holy Spirit:**
   Let us praise and exalt him above all forever!

10. **As it was in the beginning, is now, and will be forever. Amen.**
    Let us praise and exalt him above all forever!

Prayer

As in most of his prayers, Francis here addresses God under two aspects: first, the transcendent God as seen in the opening words **Almighty, most holy, most high**

and supreme; secondly, the immanent God as expressed in the word **good** repeated four times.

> **Almighty, most holy**
> **most high and supreme God,**
> **all good,**
> **supreme good,**
> **totally good,**
> **You Who alone are good,** [cf. Lk 18:19]

Although Francis rarely engages in intercessory prayer, he does so here. Nevertheless, the object of the petition is the very prayer-stance he assumes before God, asking that we be empowered to **give back to** God **all praise, glory, grace, honor, blessing and all good**.

> **may we give back to You**
> **all praise,**
> **all glory,**
> **all grace,**
> **all honor,**
> **all blessing,** [Rev 4:9,11; 5:12]
> and all good.

The conclusion of this prayer with its repetition of **so be it** *(fiat)* taken from Ps 40:14 and its equivalent **Amen** stresses the earnestness of his petition.

> So be it.
> **So be it.** [Ps 40:14]
> **Amen.**

In a certain sense we might say that this triple **Amen** parallels the triple **Holy, Holy, Holy** at the beginning of this hymn, and like two bookends, gives to this ensemble an inclusive structure.

Antiphon

Introduction

According to liturgical practice, this *Antiphon* introduces each psalm of Francis. In his *Office of the Passion*, the *Antiphon* is intimately related to the mystery which unfolds therein.

Commentary

The first phrase of the *Antiphon* reproduces the theme of Elizabeth's salutation in the gospel of Lk 1:42: "Blessed are you among women. . . ."

> **Holy Virgin Mary,**
> **there is no one like you born in the world among women. . .**

Immediately, this contextual reference associates Mary with the mystery recalled in the texts of Francis' Little Office. What follows accentuates the Trinitarian aspect:

> . . . Daughter and Handmaid of the most high,
>   sovereign King, the heavenly Father,
> Mother of our most holy Lord Jesus Christ,
> Spouse of the Holy Spirit . . .

Mary is first of all that Daughter of Israel who was completely receptive in her answer to the angel Gabriel:

> Behold the handmaid of the Lord. May it be done to me according to your word [Lk 1:38].

Commentary

According to the promise of the angel, the Holy Spirit as Spouse would come upon her and the power of the Most High would overshadow her. She would conceive him to whom she would give birth, **our most holy Lord Jesus Christ.**

The Trinitarian expressions of the *Antiphon* introduce the principle actors of the geste sung about in the psalms of Francis' Office. First **the heavenly Father** who is **the most high, sovereign King;** then **Christ** to whom Francis gives the title **our most holy Lord.** With regard to the Holy Spirit's presence in the psalms of Francis, it will only be implicit except for one instance.

The *Antiphon* continues in the form of a prayer of intercession, the only one found in Francis' writings addressed to someone other than God:

> **Pray for us**
> **with St. Michael the archangel**
> **and with all the powers of the heavens**
> **and with all the saints**
> **together with your most holy beloved Son,**
> **Lord and Teacher.**

The expression **Pray for us** remains in this instance without specification of object. At first glance, one could recognize here a request of intercession *in favor of* the petitioner(s). One should, however, read this expression in the light of his *Earlier Rule* 23:5 to discover a more ample and original meaning. There Francis, after having given thanks to the Father, first for who the Father is, then for the work of creation, incarnation and redemption, and for the work of salvation to come, goes on to say:

Antiphon

> And because all of us miserable creatures and sinners are not worthy to say your name, we submissively pray that our Lord Jesus Christ, your beloved Son, in whom you were well-pleased, in union with the Holy Spirit, the Paraclete, give you thanks as it pleases you and him for everything.

To this action of Christ and the Spirit giving thanks to the Father, Francis in the same *Earlier Rule* 23:6 associates Mary, the angels—especially St. Michael—and all the saints according to the same structure he used in the *Antiphon*:

> We humbly pray the glorious Mother, most blessed Mary ever virgin, blessed Michael, Gabriel and Raphael and all the choirs of the blessed seraphim . . . angels, archangels, blessed John the Baptist . . . the blessed patriarchs, prophets . . . and all the saints . . . that they may give you thanks.

All this seems to indicate that for Francis, the Virgin, the angels and the saints pray **together with** Christ. Therefore, in the *Antiphon* Francis sustains the praise perspective already initiated in the *Praises*.

The mention of **the powers of the heavens** and of **St. Michael the Archangel** function to some extent as a prelude to the struggle the Hero will have to sustain against the Prince and the powers of this world.

The *Antiphon* concludes with a recall of a gospel scene of great significance for Francis, namely the washing of the disciples' feet by Jesus, who at the end of this action, says to them:

Commentary

> Do you know what I have done for you? You call me **Teacher** and **Lord**, and rightly so, for indeed I am. If I, therefore, the **Lord and Teacher**, have washed your feet, you ought to wash one another's feet. I have given you an example so that as I have done for you, you should also do [Jn 13:12–15].

In giving to Christ the title **Lord and Teacher**, the conclusion of the *Antiphon* well situates the Hero of the geste as the **Teacher** of whom Francis is an attentive disciple and as the **Lord** who has come "not to be served but to serve and give his life as a ransom . . . " [Mt 20:28].

This attitude of service is really what Francis' psalms are all about. At the end of his mission, the victorious Lamb acclaimed by all of creation in the *Praises*, the One sent by the Father, gives an account to the One who sent him. In light of this, the psalms of Francis are essentially an evocation of the various moments of the struggle against the Prince of this world which the Hero had to sustain so as to re-establish the lordship of God over creation.

Blessing–Dismissal

Introduction

The rubrics or notations contained in the various manuscripts of Francis' Little Office indicate that he always concluded this Little Office with the a *Blessing-Dismissal*.

Commentary

> *V/* **Let us bless the Lord, the living and true God.**
>
> *R/* **Let us always give back to Him praise, glory, honor, blessing and every good.**
>
> *V/* **Amen. Amen.**
>
> *R/* **So be it. So be it.**

In this short closing text, Francis characteristically expands the verse and rewords the response which traditionally conclude the canonical offices:

> *V/* Let us bless the Lord *(Benedicamus Domino)*.
>
> *R/* Let us give thanks to God *(Deo gratias)*.

He may possibly be imitating the verse and response in the final double affirmations:

> *V/* **Amen. Amen.**
>
> *R/* **So be it. So be it.**

Variable Components of the Office: The Psalms of Francis

Prelude

The psalms of Francis can be compared to a musical composition and, in this respect, can be classified into two groups. The first seven expose the main theme (the story line of the geste and the acclamation of the Hero), while the others either modulate variations on the theme or introduce complementary motifs. This approach suggests the following compositional structure:

1. **The Main Theme: The Story Line of the Hero's Geste**

    PsF 1: Gethsemane
    PsF 2: The Encounter with the Sanhedrin (the religious trial)
    PsF 3: A Morning Interlude
    PsF 4: The Encounter with the Imperial Authority (the political trial)
    PsF 5: On the Cross
    PsF 6: The Passage from this World to the Father (Death and Glorification)
    PsF 7: The Acclamation of the Hero

2. The Easter Variations

> PsF 8: Echoes of Gethsemene
> PsF 9: The New Song

3. The Festive Variations

> PsF 10: A Shout of Joy
> PsF 11: A Cry of Hope
> PsF 12: A Child's Prayer

4. The Advent Motif

> PsF 13: A Time of Expectation
> PsF 14: A Vision of Fulfillment

5. The Christmas Motif

> PsF 15: The Hero's Origins and Birth

THE FIRST SERIES
The Main Theme: The Hero's Geste

Liturgical Hour	Compline	Matins-Lauds	Prime	Terce	Sext	None	Vespers
PsF	1	2	3	4	5	6	7

In the first seven psalms of Francis the Hero recounts his combat with the Enemy, the Prince of this world. Each psalm evokes an episode of this encounter, beginning with the Hero's prayer vigil at Gethsemane, continuing with his appearances before the religious and civic courts of his day, and ending with his victory, glorification and acclamation by all of creation.

The commentaries on these texts—especially PsF **1**, **2**, **4** and **6**—will highlight the close relationship which exists between them and the gospel narratives of the Passion.

As indicated in the Introduction to these commentaries, Francis extensively reworked the psalms of this series. The number of verses which compose each psalm is generally a multiple of four. This would indicate that they were initially put together on the basis of quatrains. However, it seems that in most cases, Francis abandoned this mold to express more freely his ever-deepening grasp of the geste of his Hero.

Francis initially composed these seven psalms for Passiontide: Good Friday and Holy Saturday. But he also prayed them on weekdays during Ordinary Time after Pentecost and after Epiphany, as well as during Lent.

Gethsemane

*For Compline
on Good Friday and Holy Saturday
on weekdays during Ordinary Time and during Lent*

Introduction

In his first psalm Francis begins the geste by introducing the actors: the Hero-Narrator, God the Father, the enemies (who act on behalf of the Enemy, the Prince of the world), and the Hero's friends and companions who quickly disappear from the action. The setting of the psalm is Gethsemane where the Hero spends the night before the battle in a vigil of prayer, as did all heroes of medieval gestes. Francis begins with Compline of Holy Thursday because, as it says in the opening rubric of the psalms, "on that night the Lord Jesus Christ was betrayed and taken captive."

As indicated in the Introduction to these commentaries, most of Francis' psalms are constructed on the basis of quatrains, groups of four verses. In the case of PsF 1, three verses—1, 5, 9—beginning with an invocation addressed to God the Father, signal its structure: two quatrains—verses 1-4 and 5-8—completed by a two-verse refrain—9-10.

Setting: Gethsemane.
Focus: "Your will be done."

(Christ the Hero addresses the Father.)

Commentary

1. **O God, I have given you an account
    of my life;
    you have placed my tears in your sight.**
    [Ps 55:8b–9]

Why did Francis choose this specific starting point? Very possibly because of the Latin verb *nuntiavi* (**I have given an account**) which calls to mind the action of a *nuntius* (nuncio), that is, one who is sent by someone else to accomplish a mission. The verb *nuntiare* qualifies the action of the nuncio giving an account of his mission. Here the Latin has a very interesting sequence that may have impressed Francis. It begins with the word **God** *(Deus)*, then **my life** *(vitam meam)* and finally, **I have given an account** *(nuntiavi)*. Immediately one recognizes a plan. **God** is the person whom the Hero addresses. What the Hero says concerns his **life**. And he specifies what he is going to do, that is, **give an account**. This, then, is an introductory verse to the

Psalm 1

whole saga in which the nuncio is to give an account of his life-mission to the One who sent him.

The second part of the verse already announces the difficulty of this mission. There is a question of **tears** that the Hero shed during the mission. Here Francis most likely follows the lead of Heb 5:7–8, where it is said of Christ that

> in the days of his flesh, having offered up prayers and pleas with loud cries and **tears** to God who was able to deliver him from death, was answered because of this reverence (which will be recalled in PsF 2:6). Even though he was the Son of God, through what he suffered, he learned *obedience.*

For his opening verse Francis used Ps 55:8b–9, but Ps 55:10 is not encountered until verse 6 of his psalm. There Ps 55:10 evokes the moment when the enemies turn back and fall to the ground, which correlates with what one finds in Jn 18:4–7:

> Jesus, knowing everything that was going to happen to him, went out and said to them: "Whom are you looking for?" They answered him: "Jesus the Nazarene." Jesus said to them: "I am." ... When he said to them, "I am," they turned away and fell to the ground.

Consequently, Francis has an appropriate introduction to a full account of the saga as well as an evocation of a precise moment in the first phase of that saga. So in verses 2–5 of his psalm he introduces the listener to the unfolding events that bring the Hero to that moment in verse 6 where the enemies fall to the ground. He builds up momentum by starting with **evil thoughts** conjured up by the enemies as written in following verse:

> 2. **All my enemies were conjuring evil thoughts against me; they took counsel together.** [Ps 40:8a; 70:10c]

In verse 2 Francis gets his cue from Mt 26:3–4, where Matthew introduces the plot against Jesus with the chief priests and the elders of the people who gathered and **took counsel together** in order to arrest and kill Jesus. Francis found verse 2 already compiled of material taken from Ps 40:8a and 70:10c in a liturgical verse from Matins of Passion Sunday. At first the enemies' opposition is interior, springing from evil thoughts—thinking or **conjuring evil thoughts against me**. From that starting point, Francis builds the momentum of the opposition the Hero will have to face in the course of his mission. This opposition finds its expression in verse 3:

> 3. **And they put up evil against me for good, and hatred for my love.** [Ps 108:5]

The choice of this verse taken from Ps 108:5 seems to have been called to Francis' mind by the bridge words **evil** and **against me** found in both verses 2 and 3 of his psalm. Verse 3 initiated a gradation in the opposition, moving from **evil for good** to **hatred for love**. The peak of this gradation one finds in his verse 4a:

> 4a. **For the reason for which they should have loved me, they slandered me;** [Ps 108:4a]

Psalm 1

To better follow the gradation, Francis inverted verses 4 and 5 of Ps 108. Here Francis echoes Jn 15:25, where Jesus says: "They have hated me without a cause." This has to be interpreted in the light of the earlier verse: "Whoever hates me hates my Father also" [Jn 15:23]. After this description of the enemies' actions against the Hero, Francis uses the second part of verse 4 of Ps 108 to introduce his Hero's reaction:

4b. **but I prayed:** [Ps 108:4b]

*

The hero's reply to this opposition is to contact through prayer the One who sent him:

5. **"My holy Father, King of heaven and earth, be not far from me;
for tribulation is near and there is no one to help me.** [Mt 26:42; Jn 17:11; Ps 21:12]

This prayer on the part of Jesus refers to the situation described in Mt 26:39ff, where Jesus goes to Gethsemane with three disciples and prays prostrate on the ground, saying: "**My Father**, if it is possible, let this cup pass from me; yet not what I want but what you want." After the opening words (**My Father**) taken from Matthew's narrative, Francis turns to Ps 21:12 which is introduced in verse 11 by the expression "From the womb I was projected into you." This evokes the idea of total dedication to the Father by being projected into the Father's will. In Gethsemane, according to Francis, Jesus "placed his will into the will of the Father" [2LtF 10], mimicking the medieval feudal ritual where serfs swore fealty to their lord by placing their hands in the hands of the lord. Ps 21:12, which becomes most of verse 5 of Francis' psalm, says: **be not far from me, for tribulation is near and there is no one to help me**. But in his psalm after having quoted the first words of Jesus at Gethsemane (**My Father**), Francis continues with additions taken from Jn 17:11 (**holy Father**) and Ps 5:3 (**my King**): **My holy Father, King of heaven and earth**.

Then the Hero's prayer continues with the verse already mentioned, taken from Ps 55:10, recalling the enemies falling to the ground, according to Jn 18:4–7:

> 6. **Let my enemies turn back on whatever day**
>   **I shall call upon you";**
>   **behold, I knew that you are my God.**
>   [Ps 55:10]

In the second part of verse 6, Francis stresses the human nature of the Hero by having him experience the presence of God in that very moment of his mission: **behold, I knew that you are my God**. The scene in Jn 18:4–7, referred to above, continues as Jesus says to the soldiers who came to arrest him: "If you are looking for me, let these men go," indicating his disciples. This gospel text prompts Francis to continue his psalm by mentioning the Hero's friends and companions:

> 7. **My friends and my companions drew near**
>   **and stood against me;**
>   **and my neighbors stayed far from me.**
>   [Ps 37:12]

The expression **against me**, already used to qualify the attitude of the Hero's enemies in verses 2 and 3, suggests a similar attitude on the part of **friends and companions** in this situation. The opening words **my friends** and the concluding phrase **far from me** of verse 7, become for Francis a bridge to his next verse, in which he uses the same expressions but combines them together:

> 8. **You kept my friends far from me,
>   they made me an abomination to
>   themselves;
>   I have been handed over
>   and I was not able to escape.**
>   [Ps 89:7]

The second part of this verse suggests the actions of the soldiers arresting and binding Jesus as described in Jn 18:12: "So the band of soldiers, the tribune, and the Jewish guards seized Jesus and bound him." And it was from this anti-climactic position that the Hero continued alone his mission or geste by turning to the Father:

*

> 9. **Holy Father, do not keep your aid
>   far from me;
>   my God, see to my assistance!**
>   [Jn 17:11; Ps 21:20]

This verse introduces the refrain [vv. 9–10] which Francis will use also in PsF 4 and with variation in PsF 2 and 5. This refrain in a prayer form echoes the prayer of verse 5, which also begins with the expression **Holy Father**. In both cases, there is the request that the Father remain not . . . **far from me** [v. 9] in contrast with the

COMMENTARY

friends and companions who are in fact, **far from me** [vv. 7–8]. The second part of verse 9, **my God, see to my assistance**, expresses a surrender to the Father as if Jesus were saying: "You see to it!" This induces Francis to look for a similar concluding plea for his refrain. And he gets it from Ps 37:23 where the **Holy Father**, invoked by the Hero, is affirmed to be the **Lord, God of** *his* **salvation**:

10. **Make haste to help me,**
    Lord, God of my salvation! [Ps 37:23]

The Hero is, therefore, already conscious of the fact that salvation can only come from the One to whom he prays, namely, the **Holy Father** from whom he received his mission.

Encounter with the Sanhedrin

*For Matins-Lauds
on Good Friday and Holy Saturday
on weekdays during Ordinary Time and during Lent*

Introduction

Francis assures continuity between PsF 1 and PsF 2 by introducing his second psalm with the same invocation he had used to conclude his first psalm: **Lord, God of my salvation**. This first verse introduces two prayers said by the Hero: one in the **night** as the Hero appears before the Sanhedrin [PsF 2], the other during the **day** as he appears before Pilate [PsF 4]. The conclusion of PsF 1 saw Jesus arrested in Gethsemane and as Mt 26:57 says: "Then those who had seized Jesus led him to Caiaphas, the high priest, where the scribes and the elders had gathered."

A quatrain structure is less visible here than in other psalms of Francis. However, one notices that the beginning of verse 9 (**O God**) echoes the call of verse 1: **Lord,**

God. . . . Also verse 5 could introduce a second quatrain by restating the theme of the **mother** which first appears in verse 4.

Setting: The high priest's house.
Focus: ". . . his own people did not receive him."

(Christ the Hero addresses the Father.)

Commentary

1. **Lord, God of my salvation,**
   day and night I cried out before you.
   [Ps 87:2]

As mentioned above, this verse serves to introduce both PsF 2 and PsF 4. PsF 2 presents **night** as the context of the prayer that permeates the Hero's encounter with religious justice. This theme of **night** was most likely suggested to Francis by the gospel of John for whom **night** is a symbol of evil. After Jesus had announced that the time had come when "the Prince of this world will be thrown out" [Jn 12:31], he went on to say: "The light is with you for a little longer. Walk while you have the light, lest the darkness overtake you" [Jn 12:35]. During the Last Supper when Satan "entered into" Judas [Jn 13:27] and he left the upper room to betray his Master, John notes: "and it was **night**" [Jn 13:30].

As **night** advanced, darkness continued its work. He who is "the light of the world" [Jn 8:12] was led before the assembly of those who have been blinded by Satan—the Enemy—and who now are about to accomplish the works of their father [cf. Jn 8:41–44]. And it

PSALM 2

was with prayer that the Hero engaged in this first confrontation of hand-to-hand combat with the Enemy:

2. **May my prayer enter into your sight;
   incline your ear to my request.**
   [Ps 87:3]

3. **See to my soul and liberate it,
   because of my enemies all over me.**
   [Ps 68:19; Ps 29:2]

The Hero, now alone, is surrounded by **enemies**. His need of help is obvious and he bases his request for help [cf. vv. 2–3] on his total dependence upon the Father:

4. **Since it is you who drew me
     from the womb,
   you, my hope from my mother's breasts,
   from the womb I was projected into you.**
   [Ps 21:10–11a]

*

5. **From my mother's womb you are my God;
   do not move away from me.**
   [Ps 21:11b–12]

Verses 4 and 5 introduce the theme of the **mother**. As Francis had already suggested in the *Antiphon* **Holy Virgin Mary**, he instinctively associates Mary with the mission of her Son. The appearance of this lunar figure of the **mother** in such a **night** of suffering, while the solar figure of the Father is eclipsed until the final "Why have you abandoned Me?" [Mt 27:46], brings a glimpse of tenderness to this experience. By means of this maternal figure, Francis established a link between this **night** of darkness and the one in which the Hero was born, the **night** where for the first time, "The light shines in the darkness, and the darkness did not grasp it" [Jn 1:5]. This verb "grasp," which Francis read in Latin *(comprehendere)*, carries the meaning of "apprehending," but more so, the meaning of "comprehending." The children of darkness had, with military might, *apprehended* the Hero, but without *comprehending* the real nature of his mission.

When the high priest interrogated the Hero on the subject of his disciples and teaching, the Hero answered: "I have spoken to the world in broad daylight. . . . I have said nothing in secret" [Jn 18:20]. It is at that moment that one of the guards, acting out of the general sentiment that looked upon the Hero as an agitator, "gave Jesus a slap in the face saying: Is that how you answer the high priest?" [Jn 18:22]. Affirming the rights of the children of light, the Hero then responded: "If I have spoken wrongly, bear witness to the wrong; but if I have spoken rightly, why do you strike me?" [Jn 18:23].

The Hero's protestation must have caught Francis' attention for him to single out this very scene in his evocation of this painful encounter. He did so probably because he also had experienced the **disgrace** and the **confusion** that often results from such a situation. Francis had seen many people being humiliated, especially lepers. He will have seen in his Hero's reaction a firm protestation in favor of human dignity:

6. **You know my disgrace and my confusion and my reverence.** [Ps 68:20]

Psalm 2

This verse corresponds to Francis' preoccupation with the dignity of every person and often prompts him to underline what Christ did to return humanity its dignity. The text of the letter to the Hebrews cited previously in the commentary of PsF 1:1 throws light on **reverence** which is less easy to situate in the scene evoked than **disgrace** and **confusion**: "(Christ) in the days of his flesh, having offered up prayers and pleas with loud cries and tears to God who was able to deliver him from death, was answered because of this **reverence**" [Heb 5:7]. Use of the word **reverence** creates the heartfelt context of total submission of the Hero to the will of the Father for which reason he will be "answered." But for the moment the Hero is confronted with those who oppose the will of the Father and it is **in** (his) **sight** that the Hero, in prayer [cf. v. 2 above], encounters the Enemy who torments him **in the night** [cf. v. 1 above]:

7. **In your sight are all who trouble me;
    my heart expected disgrace and misery.**
    [Ps 68:21a–b]

The theme of compassion, to which Francis is very attentive, is inserted here as a harmonic to the theme of **mother** [cf. vv. 4–5 above]:

8. **I looked for someone who would grieve
    together with me
    and there was no one;
    and for someone who would console me
    and I found no one.**
    [Ps 68:21c–d]

*

Commentary

Therefore, the Hero alone engaged in this hand-to-hand combat with the Enemy. But the Enemy, nonetheless, sends against him numerous henchmen:

9. **O God, the wicked have risen against me,
and the synagogue of the mighty
have sought my life;
and they have not placed you in their sight.**
[Ps 85:14]

This verse furnishes the key to the interpretation of this entire psalm of Francis: **the synagogue of the mighty**, before which the Hero appeared in the **night**. In this same verse several previously-mentioned themes come together by way of repetition of similar expressions. In verse 3 above, the Hero prayed **because of** (his) **enemies all over** (him). Verse 9 makes explicit the fact that it is during his appearance before the Sanhedrin that these enemies **have risen against** (him).

In contrast with the expression **in** *God's* **sight** [cf. vv. 2, 7], one reads in verse 9 the expression **in their sight**, the sight of **the mighty** who, focusing on their own interests, make no place for God. In the sculptured artwork of Francis' time there was a very appropriate illustration of this very theme. It consisted of two female figures: one with eyes wide open represented the Church, and the other, blindfolded, represented the Synagogue. This blindness on the part of the highest tribunal of the Hero's people certainly was one of the great successes of the Prince of this world, the "father of lies" [Jn 8:44].

Psalm 2

In her canticle the Hero's mother had proclaimed that God "put down the mighty from their thrones" [Lk 1:52]. But for the moment,

> the chief priests and the whole council sought false testimony against Jesus that they might put him to death, but they found none, though many false witnesses came forward. At last two came forward. . . . But Jesus was silent. And the high priest said to him: "I adjure you by the living God, tell us if you are the Christ, the Son of God." Jesus said to him: "You have said so. But I tell you, hereafter you will see the Son of man seated at the right hand of the *power of God* and coming *on the clouds of heaven*." Then the high priest tore his robes and said: "He has blasphemed. What further witness do we still need? You have just heard the blasphemy. What is your judgment?" They answered: "He deserves death" [Mt 26:59–66].

One recognizes here the great Christ of the Roman mosaics and frescoes advancing on the clouds, holding in his hand the scroll of history, of which he is the master. The Hero knew that he would one day be associated with the "power of God." But for now **the synagogue of the mighty** has the upper hand. In their eyes the Hero, prisoner in chains, would be **free** only **among the dead**:

> 10. **I have been numbered with those who go down into the pit;
> I have become as a man without help, free among the dead.**
> [Ps 87:5–6a]

COMMENTARY

The Hero is, therefore, excluded from among the living. This image of the Excluded One, **free among the dead**, awakened in Francis profound resonances. Was it not a leper, one who was excluded from society, who had opened his eyes? Francis himself, at the beginning of his *Testament,* relates:

> The Lord gave me, brother Francis, to begin to do penance in this fashion: when I was in sin, it appeared to me extremely bitter to see lepers. And the Lord...led me among them and I experienced mercy with them. And when I took leave from them, that which appeared bitter to me was changed for me into sweetness of soul and body. [Test 1–3]

The Hero has **become as a man without help**, that is, in the eyes of the blind. But he knows on whom he can count. And, therefore, the first verse of the refrain ("My holy Father . . ."), which terminated PsF 1, is here repeated, but in an affirmative manner:

11. **You are my most holy Father,
    my King and my God.** [Ps 43:5a; Ps 88:27]

12. **Make haste to help me,
    Lord, God of my salvation.** [Ps 37:23]

In summary, then, Francis' second psalm evokes the appearance of the Hero before the representatives of the people. But blinded by the Enemy, the Prince of this world, they did not recognize him. Instead, they denounced him as an impostor and pronounced his condemnation. But Francis' Hero lived this episode in the context of a continual prayer to his Father and the **God of** (his) **salvation**.

A Morning Interlude

For Prime
during the entire year

Introduction

PsF 3 is the only psalm of Francis which serves throughout the entire liturgical year. Moreover, it does not fit in with the logical action sequence of the geste of the Hero, which is the subject of PsF 1, 2, 4, 5 and 6. Rather, PsF 3 depends on the symbolism of the hour at which it was prayed, the morning sun being a symbol of Resurrection and of victory over darkness. Therefore, it is not without links to the Hero's geste. Francis seems to have envisaged this liturgical hour as a morning interlude which opens a breach in the sorrow and sufferings the Hero is experiencing. Ps 56 fulfilled this objective and except for a verse and a half, which he replaced by Ps 17:18, Francis kept it as it stands in the book of Psalms.

PsF 3 can be divided into three quatrains.

Commentary

The backdrop for the first three verses is the night of **iniquity** during which the Hero encounters his enemies, with emphasis on his **hope** and **trust** in God:

1. **Have mercy on me, O God,**
   have mercy on me,
   for my soul trusts in you.
   [Ps 56:2a]

2. **And in the shadow of your wings**
   will I hope,
   until iniquity passes by.
   [Ps 56:2b]

Francis slightly alters the next verse of Ps 56 to underscore the fact that the **most high . . . God**, to whom the Hero will constantly cry out during his encounter with his enemies, is **my Father most holy**. The Hero's past experience of the Father's blessing is like a rock guaranteeing his hope in the Father's active presence:

3. **I will call to my Father most holy,**
   most high,
   to God who has done me good.
   [Ps 56:3]

The first quatrain ends with the proclamation of victory, thus making of this quatrain a summary of the entire geste:

4. **He sent from heaven and delivered me,**
   He disgraced those who trampled me.
   [Ps 56:4a–b]

*

Psalm 3

The opening verse of the second quatrain expands the content of verse 4. To the arrogance and hatred displayed by the enemies, God responds by sending **his mercy** and **his truth**:

5. **God has sent his mercy and his truth;
   He has snatched my soul
     from my very strong enemies
     and from those who hated me
   for they were sure [of their strength]
     over me.**
   [Ps 56:4c–5a; Ps 17:18]

God's intervention is not, therefore, a condemnation or a punishment but rather a complete reversal of the situation. The enemies, blinded by Satan, thought they had the upper-hand. Now they might be led to recognize their error and turn to God realizing that they themselves have been caught in the very **trap** they had **rigged** on the Hero's path. For God's mercy welcomes the prodigal son [cf. Lk 15:11ff] and God's truth liberates [Jn 8:32]:

6. **They rigged a trap for my feet
   and they buckled my soul.**
   [Ps 56:7a–b]

7. **They dug a pit before my face,
   and into it they have fallen.**
   [Ps 56:7c–d]

This assurance of God's victory over Satan's evildoings prompts a response of praise:

COMMENTARY

8. **My heart is ready, O God, my heart is ready,
   I will sing and chant a psalm.**
   [Ps 56:8]

*

The second quatrain had expanded upon the closing verse of the first quatrain. Similarly, the opening verse of the third quatrain echoes the praise theme of verse 8, while evoking the image of the Resurrection **at dawn**:

9. **Arise, my glory, arise psaltery and harp,
   I will arise at dawn.**
   [Ps 56:9]

This victory of the rising sun over the darkness of **night** is to be proclaimed to all nations. It is through the witness of his disciples that the Hero will **confess** and magnify God **among the peoples**:

10. **I will confess you
       among the peoples, O Lord,
    I will chant a psalm to you
       among the nations.**
    [Ps 56:10]

The Hero ends this "morning interlude" with the affirmation that his anticipated victory—**I will arise at dawn** [v. 9]—fruit of the Father's **mercy** and **truth**, is in fact a glorification of the same **most high Father** [v. 3]:

11. **For your mercy has been magnified
       even to the heavens,
    and even to the clouds your truth.**
    [Ps 56:11]

Psalm 3

12. **Be exalted above the heavens, O God,**
    and above all the earth your glory.
    [Ps 56:12]

***

Francis discovered this vision of the glorification of the Father in the gospel of John. In the scenes leading up to his Passion, Christ prayed to the Father: "Father, glorify your name" [Jn 12:28], and "Now the Son of Man is glorified and God is glorified in him" [Jn 13:31]. This vision of the Father's glorification by the Resurrection of the Son, and by the witness thereto of his disciples, could have been the motivating factor in Francis' decision of always praying PsF 3 at dawn throughout the entire liturgical year.

PSALM FOUR

Encounter with the Imperial Authority

*For Terce
on Good Friday and Holy Saturday
on weekdays during Ordinary Time and during Lent*

Introduction

As already noted in the introduction to PsF 2 which is the prayer of the **night** (**Lord . . . day and night I cried out before you**), PsF 4 refers to the events of the **day**, for the **day**'s events were also permeated by the prayer of the Hero. Here Francis relied on a traditional reference, rooted in the symbolism of the Liturgy of the Hours. For centuries the Hours of Terce (midmorning), Sext (noon) and None (mid-afternoon) were prayed respectively in relation to the condemnation before Pilate, the Crucifixion and the death of Christ.

This psalm has the same basic structure as PsF 1: eight verses evoking an episode of the Hero's geste, followed by the same two-verse refrain. One can, therefore, infer

Psalm 4

that just as in PsF 1 the first eight verses are to be interpreted as forming two quatrains, even though the text does not seem to contain any clues to this effect.

Setting: Pilate's palace.
Focus: "Then Pilate gave him up. . . ."

(Christ the Hero addresses the Father.)

Commentary

Once again Francis is guided by the gospel accounts of Matthew and John, especially from verse 3ff. of his psalm. The first two verses project an image of one who is **trampled . . . underfoot**, besieged from all sides, and an image of enemies who **all day long** are dead set against Him:

1. **Have mercy on me, O God, for man has trampled me underfoot;
he oppressed me, attacking [me] all day long.**
[Ps 55:2]

2. **All the day long my enemies have trampled me underfoot;
since numerous [were] those waging war against me.**
[Ps 55:3]

In Francis' day a common practice among commentators was to underline how, before being crucified by nails, Christ had been crucified by *tongues*. Francis, therefore, chose psalm verses which express this real-

COMMENTARY

ity: **a hateful word** [v. 3], the **counsel** the enemies took together [v. 4], the enemies **speaking among themselves** [v. 5]. Also verse 3 takes up again and amplifies the expression **against me** already found at the end of verse 2:

> 3. **All my enemies [were] against me,**
>   **they were thinking evil things of me;**
>   **they agreed upon a hateful word**
>   **against me.**
>   [Ps 40:8b–9a]
>
> 4. **Those who were guarding my life**
>   **were taking counsel together.**
>   [Ps 70:10b]
>
> *
>
> 5. **They were going outside**
>   **and were speaking among themselves.**
>   [Ps 40:7]

All this recreates very appropriately the climate of the trial before the civil authorities as reported by the gospels:

> When morning came, all the chief priests and the elders of the people took counsel against Jesus to put him to death; and after having bound him, they led him away and delivered him to Pilate the governor. . . . Pilate said to him: "Do you not hear how many things they testify against you?" [Mt 27:1–2,13].

In contrast with the flow of words from the enemies, the Hero "gave him no answer, not even to a single

Psalm 4

charge" voiced by Pilate, to the governor's great amazement [Mt 27:14]. Thus had the prophet Isaiah already foretold:

> He was offered up because it was his own will, and he opened not his mouth. He will be led as a sheep to the slaughterhouse. . . . and he will not open his mouth [Is 53:7].

On his part, John notes that those who had just pronounced Jesus guilty had led him to Pilate "to the praetorium" [Jn 18:28]. But they themselves had not entered the place, in order not to be defiled so as to be able to participate in the Passover feast. "So Pilate went out to them" [Jn 18:29], and this is echoed in verse 5 of Francis' psalm. Pilate said:

> "What accusation do you bring against this man?" They answered him: "If this man were not an evildoer, we would not have handed him over" [Jn 18:30].

Then Pilate went back into the praetorium. And in the exchange that followed, the Hero acknowledged his status as King:

> — Are you the King of the Jews?
> — Do you say this on your own, or because others have told you about me?
> — Am I a Jew? Your own people and the chief priests have turned you over to me. What have you done?
> — My kingdom is not of this world. If my kingdom were of this world, my officers would fight, that I might not be handed over to the Jews. But my kingdom is not from here.

COMMENTARY

— So you are a king?
— You say I am a king. I was born and came into the world, to bear witness to the truth. Everyone who is of the truth hears my voice [Jn 18:33–37].

At this point the governor was visibly exasperated by the course of events and blurted out: "What is truth?" [Jn 18:38]. Then he offered the crowd a choice between the Hero and Barabbas to see which of the two, according to the custom, would be set free for Passover. Barabbas was a well-known robber. The shouts of the crowd had all but submerged the Hero: "Not this one, but Barabbas!" [Jn 18:40]. Then Pilate had the Hero flogged.

Next, the governor's soldiers took Jesus into the praetorium, gathering the whole battalion before him. And they stripped him and put a scarlet robe around him. Making a crown of thorns they put it on his head and put a reed in his right hand. Kneeling before him they mocked him, saying:

> "Hail, King of the Jews!" And spitting on him, they took the reed and struck him on the head [Mt 27:27–30].

The psalm of Francis continues:

6. **All who saw me laughed at me
   and they spoke with [their] lips
   and shook [their] heads.**
   [Ps 21:8]

The derision spoken of in this verse conveys as much the choice of Barabbas by the crowd as the masquerade of homage to which the soldiers submitted the Hero.

Psalm 4

During this session of derision the enemies **spoke with [their] lips**, prolonging the crucifixion by the tongues which had been happening since the beginning of the psalm.

John continues the account of the events in the following manner:

> Pilate went out again and said to them: "Look, I am bringing him out to you that you may know that I find no crime in him." So Jesus came out wearing a crown of thorns and the purple robe. Pilate said to them: "Here is the man!" When the chief priests and the officers saw him, they cried out: "Crucify! Crucify him!" [Jn 19:4–6].

In order to convey the action, once again Francis had recourse to Ps 21. To better follow the gospel sequence, he inverts verses 7 and 8 of Ps 21 in verses 6 and 7 of his own psalm.

"Here is the man!" cried Pilate to the crowd. At the shouts of the leaders of the crowd, the Hero understood that in their eyes, he was no more a man but rather something despicable:

> 7. **But I am a worm and not a man ,**
> **the disgrace of men and an outcast**
> **of the people.**
> [Ps 21:7]

Once again a text of the prophet Isaiah is brought to mind.

> He was without attractiveness or gracefulness that we should look at him, and without beauty that we

should desire him. He was despised and the least of humanity; a person of sorrows, and acquainted with infirmity, and his face was, as it were, hidden and despicable, and we esteemed him not [Is 53:2b–3].

The Enemy, the father of lies, succeeded in his strategy. His slander had produced its effect.

When Pilate, who had found "no crime in him" [Jn 19:4], said to the crowd: "Here is your King," their cries had doubled in intensity: "Take him away! Take him away! Crucify him!" Pilate retorted: "Shall I crucify your king?" Then the high priests had decisively rejected the Hero: "We have no king but Caesar." At this point John notes tersely: "Then he handed him over to them to be crucified" [Jn 19:14–16]. To evoke this reality Francis chooses a verse which again picks up the image of **disgrace**:

8. **Far more than all my enemies,
    I have become a total disgrace
    to my neighbors
   and a dread to my acquaintances.**
    [Ps 30:12a–b]

*

PsF 4, the Hero's prayer during the events of the **day**, ends by recapturing the intensity of the refrain in its first form, that of PsF 1:9–10:

9. **Holy Father, do not keep your aid
    far from me;
   my God, see to my assistance!**
    [Jn 17:11; Ps 21:20]

Psalm 4

10. **Make haste to help me,
    Lord, God of my salvation!**
    [Ps 37:23]

The Enemy believing the objective of victory had been attained, blinded those to whom God's usurped domain had been entrusted. "Here is the heir," said the blind ones. "Come, let us kill him . . ." [cf. Mt 21:33–42]. In truth, however, the only objective the Enemy achieved was to bring the Hero to the only arena where the definitive battle could be waged.

On the Cross

For Sext
on Good Friday and Holy Saturday
on weekdays during Ordinary Time and during Lent

Introduction

Up to this point, Francis' psalms followed the sequence of events as reported by the gospels, especially Matthew and John. But PsF 5 does not follow suit. It contains a few scriptural allusions, but they do not follow the gospel order or sequence of events. Moreover, in PsF 1, 2 and 4, the Hero clearly addressed the Father. In PsF 5 one finds this possibly from verse 3ff, but more surely from verse 9ff.

This dual orientation of the psalm reveals its basic structure: two equal sections of eight verses each. These, in turn, can be subdivided into quatrains, even though as in PsF 4, the flow of images in the text does not prove helpful in this respect.

Psalm 5

Whereas PsF 1, 2 and 4 were made up of numerous citations taken from various psalms, the first six verses of PsF 5 are taken verbatim from one, Ps 141. It is known that this psalm took on great significance for Francis toward the end of his life, so much so that, as Celano writes, he recited it on his deathbed,

> . . . asking [his brothers] on his approaching death or rather, his approaching life, to sing in a loud voice with exultation of spirit the praises to the Lord (namely, the *Canticle of Brother Sun* with the new strophe on Sister Death). He himself, in as much as he could, burst out in that psalm of David: **With my voice I cried out to the Lord, with my voice I made supplication to the Lord** [1C 109].

This biographical reference corresponds quite well with the symbolism of the Liturgy of Hours, Sext being the hour when Christ was nailed to the cross, his deathbed.

In PsF 5 the Hero reviews the situation and formulates for himself the profound reasons for what is happening to him.

Setting: The Cross.
Focus: "my life . . . I freely give it up."

(Christ the Hero addresses Francis in verses 1–8, and the Father in verses 9–16.)

Commentary

In the first eight verses the Hero addresses his disciple, and immediately reminds the disciple that it was in a context of prayer that he had experienced the reality that **escape** was no longer possible:

1. **With my voice I cried out to the Lord,
   with my voice I pleaded with the Lord.**
   [Ps 141:2]

Here one detects an echo of the passage cited earlier from the letter to the Hebrews where it is said that Christ "offered up prayers and **pleas** with loud cries and **tears** to God who was able to deliver him from death. . ." and that "he learned *obedience*" [Heb 5:7–8].

2. **I pour out my prayer in his sight,
   and I voice my trouble before him.**
   [Ps 141:3]

3. **While my spirit was failing within me,
   and you, you have known my paths.**
   [Ps 141:4a–b]

It is as if Francis heard his Hero saying: "What you are going through, I endured before you." Francis, in the last days of his life, went through extremely painful trials, one of which was a spiritual trial which lasted just about two years [cf AC 21]. This trial was aggravated by internal dissension within the fraternity, centered for the most part on the subject of poverty; this dissension along with his chronic illnesses, had led Francis to abdicate the function of General Minister [cf. 2C 143; AC 76]. Similarly, the Hero also was confronted

Psalm 5

with the stance of the **arrogant** who were convinced they were right:

> 4. **On this road on which I was walking,**
>   **the arrogant have hidden a trap for me.**
>   [Ps 141:4c–d]

This text constitutes a reminder of the long road the Hero had traveled during the preceding three years, during which he had often encountered the traps cleverly set by the Scribes and the Pharisees. Finally, he was forced to drag the wood of the cross painfully to the place where he was now attached to it.

*

In vain the Hero looked for his friends:

> 5. **I looked to my right and I saw,**
>   **and there was no one who knew me.**
>   [Ps 141:5a–b]

The situation had now become irreversible. **Escape** was no longer possible:

> 6. **Escape has slipped away from me,**
>   **and there is no one who cares for my life.**
>   [Ps 141:5c–d]

Then Francis hears his Hero tell him the first reason for what the Hero is experiencing:

> 7. **For on your account**
>   **I have sustained disgrace,**
>   **confusion has covered my face.**
>   [Ps 68:8]

The consideration **on your account** must have grasped Francis' attention since he returns to it explicitly in his *Second Letter to the Faithful*:

> Such was the will of the Father that his blessed and glorious Son whom he gave to us and who was born for us, offered himself by his own blood as a sacrifice and victim...not for himself by whom all things were made, but for our sins leaving us an example that we may follow his footprints [11–13].

As the prophet had foreseen:

> Surely he has borne our grief and carried our sorrows; and we have thought him as it were a leper, and as one struck by God and afflicted. But he was wounded for our iniquities, bruised for our sins.... All we like sheep have gone astray, everyone has turned aside into his own way [Is 53:4–6].

Texts such as this are often encountered in the liturgy of Holy Week and easily would have reminded Francis of the Hero as Good Shepherd, since he himself had said:

> I am the good shepherd. The good shepherd lays down his life for the sheep.... For this reason the Father loves me, because I lay down my life, that I may take it up again. *No one takes it from me, but I lay it down of my own accord.* I have power to lay it down, and I have power to take it up again [Jn 10:11,17–18].

> No one has greater love than this, to lay down one's life for one's friends. [Jn 15:13]

Psalm 5

This idea of the Hero's giving his life for his friends seems to have become for Francis a backdrop on which the opening words of verse 7 of his psalm (**For on your account**) stand out very vividly. In fact Francis felt it was important for him and his brothers never to forget this figure of his Hero as the Good Shepherd who laid down his life for his sheep:

> And to him let us have recourse as to the shepherd and guardian of our souls, he who said: "I am the good shepherd who feeds my sheep and I lay down my life for my sheep" [ER 22:32].

The Hero adds: **on your account**, Francis,

> 8. **I have become a stranger to my brothers, and a pilgrim to the sons of my mother.** [Ps 68:9]

And Francis discovered here the perfect example of poverty to propose to his brothers at the very moment when they were discussing the topic of poverty:

> The brothers shall appropriate nothing to themselves, neither house, nor place, nor anything else. And as pilgrims and strangers in this world, serving the Lord in poverty and humility, let them go confidently for alms; and it would not be opportune for them to be ashamed because the Lord became poor for us in this world [LR 6:1–3].

Finally, the mention of the **mother** at the end of verse 8 evokes the presence of Mary at the foot of the cross, whose presence is encountered again in the next psalm of Francis.

*

COMMENTARY

Beginning with verse 9 the Hero turns from Francis to address the Father and gives the second reason for what is happening to him:

9. **Holy Father, zeal for your house
has devoured me,
and the abuses of those who have attacked
you have fallen upon me.**
[Jn 17:11; Ps 68:10]

This verse appears in John's account of the purification of the temple [Jn 2:13–21]. When the Hero had cleansed the temple area, the disciples remembered the words of the scripture: **zeal for your house has devoured me** [cf. Jn 2:17]. "The Jews then said to him: 'What sign have you to show us for doing this?' Jesus answered them: 'Destroy this temple, and in three days I will raise it up.' . . . But he spoke of the temple of his body" [Jn 2:18–19, 21].

Francis, hearing the words **zeal for your house**, cannot but recall the mission that the Hero had entrusted to him when, in the little church of San Damiano, he had called out: "Francis, go, repair my house which . . . is being totally destroyed . . ." [2C 10]. Francis had first concluded that the "house" he was to repair was the little chapel in which he found himself. Then he understood that what was meant by this "house" was the Church—the Body of Christ [cf. 1Cor 12:12ff]—made up of living stones, which was to be repaired with the mortar of gospel living. Later on, especially in his contact with the Saracens and likely with the Jews of his time, Francis discovers that this "house" of God which he has been called to repair goes beyond the confines

Psalm 5

of the Church to include all of humanity. Now the bricklayer becomes the instrument of God's peace. Finally, Francis understands that the "house" encompasses all of creation which, according to Paul, awaits the ultimate consequences of the Hero's action of reparation and restoration so as to enter also into the liberty of the children of God [cf. Rm 8:19–21]. The Hero is the "cornerstone" of the new creation, that is, all of creation which has been restored to its dignity as "house" or domain of God.

In the parable of the vineyard, the tenants to whom the owner (the Father) had entrusted his vineyard (his creation), blinded by the Enemy, wanted to kill the owner's son (the Hero) [cf. Mt 21:33–42] to have his inheritance for themselves. The Hero of Francis' geste is quite aware of the fact that his mission concerns his Father's house, his vineyard, his creation which needs to be restored and given back to its rightful owner. This is really what is at stake in this battle in which he is now irreversibly engaged. To conclude his parable of the vineyard the Hero had asked the question: "Have you never read in the scriptures: The very stone which the builders rejected has become the cornerstone?" [Mt 21:42].

And it was this affirmation of the scriptures that sustained the hope of the Hero. But for now, as he hung from the cross reviewing the events of the last hours, he was, as it were, invaded by the absurdity of the situation. He felt as if he were drowning in a sea of contradictions:

Commentary

10. **And against me they rejoiced
    and united together;
    scourges were heaped upon me
    and I knew not why.**
    [Ps 34:15]

11. **They have become more numerous
    than the hairs of my head,
    those who hate me without cause.**
    [Ps 68:5a–b]

12. **My enemies have been strengthened,
    those who persecuted me unjustly;
    then I was repaying what I did not steal.**
    [Ps 68:5c–d]

The Hero had been accused of stealing the title of "Son of God" [cf. Mt 26:63–66]. But it was the Father who had attested to this when he was baptized by his cousin John:

> After Jesus was baptized . . . the heavens were opened and he saw the Spirit of God descending like a dove, and hovering over him; and behold, a voice from heaven, saying: "This is my beloved Son, in whom I am well pleased" [Mt 3:16–17].

*

The Hero recalls the scene where witnesses had come forth to report and deform the words he had used when he chased the merchants from the temple. These merchants had made of the house of his Father a "house of trade" [Jn 2:16]. It was at that moment when speaking of his body, the Hero had assured: "*Destroy* this temple,

Psalm 5

and in three days I will raise it up" [Jn 2:19]. In effect the ancient Temple would be replaced by a new Temple—his body, and then the Church, the community of his disciples.

The absurdities were accumulating. Witnesses had declared that he had said: "*I will destroy* this temple . . . " [Mk 14:58]:

13. **Evil witnesses standing up
were interrogating me
on what I knew nothing about.**
    [Ps 34:11]

All this slander, was it not the triumph of lies? The Hero's actions and words were distorted while he was simply **pursuing goodness**:

14. **They were repaying me evil for good,
and were slandering me
because I was pursuing goodness.**
    [Ps 34:12a; 37:21]

The Hero now had to face the absurdity of the situation. He had reacted with dignity when the soldier had slapped his face. Now he felt welling up in him a strong sense of indignation. All this was so unjust. He had then reacted with composure, but he was helpless now as even **escape has slipped away from [him]**. He sensed that despair was lurking close by. This was the Enemy's last trap.

By gathering this pile of contradictions in verses 10–14, Francis found a way of transcribing in his psalm the gospel account of the Hero's impression of being abandoned by the Father: "My God, my God, why have

COMMENTARY

you forsaken me?" [Mt 27:46]. As the Hero continued praying psalm 22, he would experience his hope surfacing again in verse 19: "O Lord, **do not keep your aid far from me**; see to my defense" [cf. PsF 1:9; 4:9].

And this hope in the presence of the Father would permit him to continue with his mission:

15. **You are my most holy Father,
    my king and my God.**
    [Ps 43:5]

16. **Make haste to help me,
    Lord, God of my salvation!**
    [Ps 37:23]

After the prayer vigil [PsF 1] and the first encounters with the Enemy [PsF 2, 4], PsF 5 emerges as a pause in the action where the Hero, submerged in a sea of absurdity, convinces himself that all this makes sense because of concern for Francis and out of zeal for his Father's house. And in overcoming the last temptation, that of despair, he prepares himself for the final encounter with the Prince of this world.

Passage from This World to the Father

For None
on Good Friday and Holy Saturday
on weekdays during Ordinary Time and during Lent

Introduction

In PsF 5, the scene became more animated. Christ not only addressed the Father as in the first psalms, but also he addressed his disciple Francis [vv.1–8]. Now, in PsF 6 Christ addresses the Father in only two verses [vv.12–13]. In the remaining verses he speaks to the crowd, except for the very end of the psalm where Francis speaks for the first time [vv.15–16].

Up to this point it is the Christ in glory—the Lamb of the heavenly liturgy evoked in the *Praises*—who is heard speaking about his encounter with the Enemy. In PsF 6 the setting changes dramatically. One gets the impression of a super-imposition of the Crucified One on to the Victorious Lamb. It is as if Francis finds himself once

269

again before the crucifix of San Damiano, from which Christ had called him to repair his house and on which he now contemplates the Hero of his geste, beyond death while still nailed to the cross. The death wound of his side is clearly visible, yet his opened eyes and serene countenance attest to his victory over the forces of darkness.

Even though the various images and evocations of PsF 6 do not fall into regular sub-groups, its sixteen verses can, nevertheless, be seen as pointing to an earlier structure of four quatrains.

Setting: The Cross.
Focus: . . . Jesus knowing that his hour had come to pass from this world to the Father. . . .

(Christ the Hero addresses the people in verses 1–11, the Father in verses 12–13, again the crowd in verse 14. Francis addresses the people in verses 15–16.)

Commentary

From the cross the Hero calls out to the crowd:

1. **O all of you who pass along the way, consider and see if there is a sorrow like my sorrow.**
   [Lm 1:12a–b]

Francis surely understood this text, which is often used in the liturgy of Passiontide, as an appeal to compassion; and John tells us that "many of the Jews" read the inscription "Jesus the Nazarene, the King of the Jews" dictated by Pilate [Jn 19:19–20]:

Psalm 6

2. **For many dogs have surrounded me
   a gathering of evildoers has besieged me.**
   [Ps 21:17]

It is probable that for Francis **the way** of verse 1 does not simply apply to these witnesses of the crucifixion. It is true that PsF 5 also referred to the **road on which I was walking** [v. 4], which could signify only the way of the cross which the Hero had just trod. But if one considers that this theme will reappear in PsF 15:7 (Christ **was born for us along the way**), one is encouraged to think that for Francis **the way** mentioned at the beginning of PsF 6 is not only the way of the cross but the way of an entire lifetime of which the carrying of the cross is the culmination. Reference is, therefore, made to **the way** of everyone's entire existence. It is as if Christ were saying: **O all of you**, pilgrims of this world. On the basis of PsF 5:8 (**I have become a stranger . . . and a pilgrim. . . .**), it is probably not far from the truth to think that, at least in the mind of Francis, one cannot really empathize with Christ if one is not like Christ, a "pilgrim and stranger in this world" [ER 6:2].

After these opening verses the Hero recalls the events which preceded his death:

3. **They certainly have stared at
      and examined me;
   they have divided my garments
      among them
   and for my tunic they have cast lots.**
   [Ps 21:18b–19]

Here Francis continues to follow mostly the narratives of John and Matthew. Ps 21:17c–19 furnished him with the appropriate text, but he transposes the verses and, in the process, inverts the sequence of events recounted by the evangelists:

> So they took Jesus. . . and carrying the cross himself, he went out to what is called the Place of the Skull, in Hebrew, Golgotha where they crucified him. . . . When the soldiers had crucified Jesus, they took his garments and divided them into four shares, a share for each soldier. They also took his tunic. But the tunic was seamless, woven in one piece from the top down. So they said to one another, "Let us not tear it, but cast lots for it to see whose it will be," in order that the passage of scripture might be fulfilled that says: **they have divided my garments among them and for my tunic they have cast lots** [Jn 19:16b–18a, 23–24].

By inverting these two events, Francis may have wanted to create a certain gradation towards the actual nailing to the cross so as to emphasize it. In so doing, he recovered an equivalent of the motif of the crucifixion by tongues preceding the crucifixion by nails [cf. PsF 4:1–5]. In this instance the enemies **certainly have stared at and examined** him, piercing him with their eyes [v. 3] before the piercing of his hands and feet by the nails:

4. **They have pierced my hands and my feet; and they have counted all my bones.**
   [Ps 21:17c–18a]

*

The Hero then had to bear the insults of the crowd who derided him on the subject of the temple which he said

Psalm 6

he would rebuild in three days, and also on the subject of his title as King and Son of God:

> Those passing by reviled him, shaking their heads and saying: "You who would destroy the temple and rebuild it in three days, save yourself; if you are the Son of God, come down from the cross!" Likewise the chief priests with the scribes and elders mocking him said: "He saved others; he cannot save himself. If he is the king of Israel, let him come down from the cross now, and we will believe in him. He trusted in God; let him deliver him now if he wants him. For he said: "I am the Son of God" [Mt 27:40–43].

Deep within himself the Hero knew that the temple of his body would not be destroyed forever, and that all would one day see his glory as King and Son of God. But as he hung on the cross, he had to accept the painful reality of the disbelief of his people:

5. **They have opened their mouth against me like a ravaging and roaring lion.**
   [Ps 21:14]

And he realized that the end was near; life was gradually ebbing away from his broken body:

6. **I have been poured out like water and all of my bones have been scattered.**
   [Ps 21:15a–b]

It was at this moment that, according to John's narrative, an event took place which had made his heart **become like melting wax**; she whose discreet presence had brought him a ray of hope [PsF 2:5] was standing beneath the cross:

> When Jesus saw his mother and the disciple there whom he loved, he said to his mother: "Woman, behold your son." Then he said to the disciple, "Behold your mother" [Jn 19:26–27].

A moment of intense emotion occurs:

> 7. **And my heart has become like melting wax within my chest.**
>   [Ps 21:15c]

Afterwards events leading to the denouement accelerated:

> 8. **My strength has dried up like baked clay and my tongue has stuck to my palate.**
>   [Ps 21:16a–b]

In fact John pursues:

> After this, knowing that everything was now finished . . . Jesus said: "I thirst." There was a vessel filled with common wine. So they put a sponge soaked in wine on a branch of hyssop and put it up to his mouth [Jn 19:28–29].

Ps 68 supplied Francis with an appropriate text for this episode:

> 9. **And they have given gall as my food and in my thirst they have given me vinegar to drink.**
>   [Ps 68:22]

Psalm 6

> When Jesus had taken the vinegar, he said: "It is finished." And bowing his head, he handed over the spirit [Jn 19:30].
>
> And crying out in a loud voice, Jesus said: "Father, into your hands I commend my spirit." And saying this, he expired [Lk 23:46].

Francis had recourse to Ps 21 for a suitable verse for this death scene:

**10. And they have led me
into the dust of death;
and have added to the pain of my wounds.**
[Ps 21:16c; 68:27b]

For the second part of verse 10, Francis follows the interpretation which was commonly given to this text by putting it in relation to the events which immediately followed the death of the Hero:

> In order that the bodies might not remain on the cross on the Sabbath, for that Sabbath was indeed a solemn day, the Jews asked Pilate that their legs be broken and they be taken down. So the soldiers came and broke the legs of the first and then of the other one who was crucified with him. But when they came to Jesus, seeing that he was already dead, they did not break his legs, but one of the soldiers pierced his side with a lance . . . [Jn 19:31–34].

At this point in Francis' psalm the whole situation changes because it is at this very moment that the Hero is locked in body-to-body combat with the Enemy, combat to the finish. He finally encounters the Enemy on the battlefield where the Enemy's victory seems indisputable, namely, death. Even if the psalm is composed for Good Friday, the day which focuses on the death of Christ, Francis cannot stop the dynamics of the drama because it is at this very moment that his Hero gives his victorious deathblow to the Enemy. Francis' text mirrors the vision of John in whose gospel, to be "exalted above the earth" (on the cross: where human impotence reaches its apex) corresponds to the moment when, entering into his glory, Christ acquires the power of drawing all things to himself:

> The hour has come for the Son of Man to be glorified. . . . Now is the judgment of the world; now the Prince of this world will be driven out. And when I am exalted above the earth, I will draw everything to myself. He said this indicating the kind of death he would die [Jn 12:23,31–33].

As Christ goes to the very limit of taking upon himself sinful humanity in all its poverty, at that very moment he resurrects. Or rather, at this moment the Father, in whom he has placed all his trust, raises him. This is the hour of his glorification, the hour of the defeat of the Enemy, the Prince of this world. From this moment on, the Hero is the new Master of the house of God:

> 11. **I have slept. . .and I have resurrected,**
> **And my most holy Father**
> **has received me with glory.**
> [Ps 3:6; 72:24c]

Until this point, the Hero recounted the various phases of his mission. In the first verses of PsF 6 he addressed the crowd. Now he turns towards him whom he has

Psalm 6

recognized as the **God of** his **salvation**, his **holy Father**:

(Christ addresses the Father.)

> 12. **Holy Father, you have held my right hand and according to your will you have led me and have lifted me up with glory.**
> [Jn 17:11; Ps 72:24]

In the letter to the Hebrews one reads: "Behold, I come. At the beginning of the book it is written of me that I accomplish, O God, your will" [Heb 10:7]. At each moment of his life the Hero could say: "My food is to do the will of the one who sent me and to complete his work" [Jn 4:34]. Or again: "I came down from heaven not to do my own will but the will of the one who sent me. And this is the will of the one who sent me, that I should not lose anything of what he gave me" [Jn 6:38–39].

The Hero had been the servant of the Father's project:

> Though he was in the form of God,
> he did not regard equality with God
> something to be grasped.
> Rather, he emptied himself,
> accepting the form of a slave,
> being made in human likeness;
> and found human in appearance,
> he humbled himself,
> becoming obedient to death,
> even death on a cross.
> Because of this, God exalted him
> and gave him the name

which is above every name,
so that at the name of Jesus
every knee should bend,
of those in heaven and on earth
and under the earth,
and every tongue confess that
Jesus Christ is Lord,
to the glory of God the Father.
[Phil 2:6–11]

His obedience had made him the slave of all; God made him the Lord of all. It is really the Father who, according to his will, led the Hero throughout his entire difficult mission:

13. **For what is there in heaven for me,**
   and besides you,
   what have I wanted on earth?
   [Ps 72:25]

Now the victorious Hero addresses the crowd and in the face of those who refused him the title, he proclaims:

(Christ addresses the people.)

14. **Behold, behold, for I am God,**
   says the Lord . . .

It is in effect the Father—**the Lord**—who proclaims that the Hero is God, according to what is written in Ps 2:7: "The Lord said to me: 'You are my son; today I have begotten you.'"

The humanity of Christ now opens its eyes on its divine dimension. This man, Jesus of Nazareth [cf. Acts

Psalm 6

2:22] knew himself to be Son of God, but did not yet know all that this implied. This phrase **Behold, behold, for I am God** leaves one with the impression of Christ the Hero being overwhelmed by the marvels of an extraordinary reality.

This is in line with Ps 2:8, which continues:

> Ask of me and I will give you the nations for an inheritance and the ends of the earth for possession,

and the Hero adds:
> **. . . I shall be exalted among the nations
> and I shall be exalted on the earth.**
> [Ps 45:11]

And so ends the Hero's narrative, emphasizing the universal dimension of his mission.

Then Francis enters the scene and, confessing the divinity of the Hero as well as his new title of **Lord**, offers thanks for the great deed which has been accomplished in favor of the servants of the Lord and of all who put their hope in him:

(Francis addresses the people.)

> 15. **Blessed be the Lord, the God of Israel,
> who has redeemed the souls of his servants
>   with his own most holy blood
> and who will not abandon
>   all who hope in him.**
> [Lk 1:68a; Pss 71:18; 33:23; Heb 9:12]

The Hero was judged, condemned and put to death by the justice of those who had been blinded by the "father of lies," who "was a murderer from the beginning" [cf. Jn 8:44]. But Francis knows that the Hero, now established as Lord before whom "every knee should bend, of those in heaven and on earth and under the earth" [Phil 2:10], will judge this erroneous justice:

> 16. **And we know that he comes,
> that he will come to judge justice.**
> [1Jn 5:20; Ps 95:13b; 74:3]

This is the foundation of Francis' hope; he *knows* that the justice that condemns the just will in turn be condemned.

And so ends this psalm assembled by Francis for the hour of None, which traditionally commemorates the death of Christ. His insight into the majestic vision of Christ coming on the clouds, an image which Francis had been able to contemplate in the churches of Rome, shows that in his contemplation of the mystery of the cross he recaptures the vision which the Fathers of the Church had of this mystery. It is the vision of the glorious cross, the Paschal cross, from which the victory of God over the forces of evil and death bursts forth.

Acclamation of the Hero

*For Vespers
during the entire year
except the Christmas Season*

Introduction

PsF 6 was permeated with the logic of John the Evangelist's unified vision of the death-resurrection-glorification event. PsF 7, even for Passiontide, centers around the entire creation's acclamation of the Hero, its new King, and the joy of his victory.

The three quatrain structure of this psalm is underlined by the parallel invitations of verses 1, 5 and 9:

- **All you peoples clap your hands . . .**
- **Sing to [the Lord] a new song . . .**
- **Let the whole earth be moved. . . .**

(Francis addresses the people.)

Commentary

At the end of PsF 6, Francis briefly entered the scene to acclaim the Hero. Now he assumes the role of a Master of Ceremonies: "Good people—*Buona gente*—(one of Francis' favorite expressions when addressing a crowd), the geste is ended. Let's hear a good round of applause for the Hero!"

> 1. **All you peoples clap your hands;**
>   **raise to God a shout of joy**
>   **with a voice of exultation.**
>   [Ps 46:2]

The Latin word used here for **peoples** *(gentes)* is quite close to the Italian word for the crowd *(la gente)*. Consequently one can understand that for Francis, it is all who hear the geste, and ultimately **all who pass along the way** of life and who were called upon at the beginning of PsF 6 (**Oh all you who pass along the way**), that are now invited to applaud and rejoice. After the **tears** the cries of **joy**!

The victorious Hero makes his entry. This situation is now the opposite to that of the scene with Pilate [cf. PsF 4:7; Jn 19:15]: "This is *your king*! . . . Take him away! take him away! Crucify him!" *(Tolle, Tolle. . .)*

The truth has now been re-established. Therein lies the cause of all this rejoicing :

> 2. **Because the Lord [is] the Most High,**
>   **the awesome, great King over all the earth.**
>   [Ps 46:3]

Psalm 7

Here is the "Great King" for whom Francis had wanted to be the "herald" by his entire life. He realized this heraldic role more vividly in these psalms, which he "arranged in reverence, memory and praise of the (glorious) Passion of the Lord," as noted by the scribes who copied his psalms.

Then Francis acknowledges that the One at the origin of the geste is the Father to whom the Hero, in the preceding psalms, had unceasingly prayed and given an account of his mission:

3. **For the most holy Father of heaven,
   our King before all ages,
sent his beloved Son from on high,
and brought about salvation
   in the center of the earth.**
   [Ps 73:12; 143:7; Mt 17:5; Jn 3:17; Gal 4:4]

Just as the Father is **King before all ages**, the Son also is **King over all the earth** [v. 2]. Francis was sensitive to the fact that the Father **sent his beloved Son** "not to condemn the world, but so that through him the world may be saved" [Jn 3:17]. Through the Son the Father **brought about salvation in the center of the earth**. The image here is that of the cross as the Tree of Life planted in the center of the "new earth" [Rev 21:1]. A well known legend in Francis' time stated that the cross of Christ was planted on the very spot where Adam was buried. Consequently, **the most holy blood** of Christ [PsF 6:15], dripping from his wounds, would first cleanse the father of fallen humanity. At a later date this legend would inspire artists to include Adam's skull at the foot of the cross.

In fact, the Hero's victory is to benefit all of creation; that which had been "made subject to vanity... will be liberated from the servitude of corruption to enter into the liberty of the glory of the children of God" [Rm 8:20–22]:

4. **Let heavens rejoice and earth exult,
   let the sea and all that is in it be moved.
   let fields and all that is in them be glad.**
   [Ps 95:11–12a]

This first quatrain proclaims that the parable of the murderous tenants [Mt 21:33ff; cf. PsF 5:9] has found its ultimate conclusion, namely, that even as he is put to death, the owner's Son has saved the domain. Salvation has come to all of creation, God's domain and house.

*

The second quatrain opens with a return to the theme of the acclamation of the Lord-King:

5. **Sing to him a new song;
   sing to the Lord, all the earth!**
   [Ps 95:1]

In Scripture, the **new song** accompanies each one of God's great deeds. But since the creation of the world, no other great deed has equaled the Hero's victory over the Prince of this world and his acolytes. Thinking of themselves as **gods**, they had imposed themselves **all over** the Hero [PsF 2:3] by usurping the authority and the power which belong solely to God and to the Lamb [*Praises*]. As a result, the Hero had become **a total dis-**

grace [PsF 5:8]. But now he is **Lord, great and highly to be praised** and **worthy of awe above all** these **gods**:

6. **For the Lord is great
    and highly to be praised;
    worthy of awe above all gods.**
    [Ps 95:4]

During the Hero's trial, the crowd had rejected him declaring: "We have no king but Caesar!" [Jn 19:15]. Now the crowd is invited to acknowledge *him* as the new King. Having received **power and divinity and wisdom and strength**, the Lamb is now worthy **to receive honor and glory and blessing** [*Praises* 3]:

7. **Bring to the Lord, families of nations,
    bring to the Lord glory and honor,
    bring to the Lord the glory due his name.**
    [Ps 95:7–8a]

He has indeed received **the name** which is above every name [cf. Phil 2:9] and there is no other name by which all may be saved [cf. Acts 4:12]. He is the **Lord and Teacher** [*Antiphon*] who has set forth the *example* so all may do as he did [cf. Jn 13:15]. Consequently, the homage to the new King ends with a call to follow him **along the way** [PsF 6:1] on which he walked so as to arrive where he now is, in the glory of the Father:

8. **Reject your bodies
    and take up his holy cross;
    and follow his most holy commands
    to the very end.**
    [Ps 95:8b; Mt 16:24; 10:22; cf. Jn 15:10]

COMMENTARY

The interpretation of the first words of this verse (**Reject your bodies**) is somewhat complicated by the fact that Francis makes use of a Latin verb *tollite* which carries two contrasting meanings: first, "reject" or "cast off," and secondly, "take up" or "offer up."

On the basis of Ps 95 which Francis quoted in the preceeding verses, one can argue in favor of "take up" (or "offer up") **your bodies**. But as the verse continues, one senses that Francis contrasts the **bodies** with the Hero's **holy cross** which all are invited to **take up** (*bajulare*). Moreover, the verb *tollere* is also the expression used by the crowd to reject the "king" that Pilate presented to them: "Take him away!" *(Tolle!)* [cf. commentary above for PsF 7:1]. And it is this last meaning of *tollite* that seems to best suit the general thrust of verse 8: **Reject your bodies**. But here the word "body" is taken in the Pauline sense of the selfish, sinful self ("the *old* self" of Eph 4:22), which is also commonly encountered in Francis' writings, especially in his *Second Letter to the Faithful*:

> *We should hate our **bodies** with their vices and sins, for the Lord says in the gospel: all evils, vices, and sins come from the heart. . . . We should deny ourselves* and *put our **bodies** under the yoke* of service and holy obedience. . . .
>
> We should not be wise and prudent according to the flesh, but rather, simple, humble and pure. And we should *hold our **bodies** in contempt and scorn,* for all of us, through our own fault, are miserable and rotten, fetid and (we are) worms, as the Lord says through the prophet: **I am a worm and not a man,**

Psalm 7

the disgrace of men and an outcast of the people.
[2LtF 37, 40, 45–46; cf. PsF 4:7]

Francis makes a significant change in the scriptural material which he uses. In the gospels the disciple is invited to **take up** *his/her* (personal) **cross** and follow Christ. In PsF 7:8, the listener is invited to **take up his** (that is, Christ's) **holy cross**. The reference here can only be to Simon of Cyrene, who according to Lk 23:36, carried Jesus' cross on the way to Calvary. Therefore, in Francis' view, rejection of the **bodies** (the "old self") is not just a negative act, but above all the necessary condition for a positive attitude, namely, that each one has to become as Simon, a cross-bearer for those with whom Jesus identified himself when he proclaimed: "As long as you did it for one of these my lesser brothers, you did it for me" [Mt 25:40].

As the Hero himself had expressed it as he hung on his own cross [cf. PsF 5], compassionate love of neighbor and love of God were indeed the basis of the Law and the Prophets [cf.Mt 22:40]. Moreover, as the apostle John reminds us, is not one's love of the neighbor whom one sees the test of one's love for God whom one does not see [cf. 1 Jn 4:20]?

For the rest of verse 8 (**take up his holy cross and follow his most holy commands even to the end**) Francis drew material from various New Testament texts, such as:

- If someone wants to come after me, let him *renounce himself*, **take up** *his* **cross** and follow me [Mt 16:24];
- Whosoever does not *carry his* **cross** . . . cannot be my disciple [Lk 14:27];

- Christ has suffered for you, leaving you an *example*, so that you may **follow** his footsteps [1Pt 2:21];
- If you **follow** my **commands**, you will remain in my love . . . [Jn 15:10];
- You will be despised by all because of my name; but he who *perseveres* **even to the end**, will be *saved* [Mt 10:22].

Finally, Francis' own experience—as often expressed in his writings—had tested the truth of the Hero's teaching, namely, that the quality of discipleship can be proved only when it is submitted to the test of time (**follow his . . . commands even to the end**). Only then does it become visible that the seed of the Word has fallen on "good ground" [ER 22:17; Lk 8:15].

So without any moralizing emphasis, Francis ends the second quatrain of his psalm by spelling out in verse 8 the demanding moral of his Hero's geste.

During Advent this psalm ends here.

That Francis would end PsF 8 here during Advent likely points to the fact that this psalm originally ended with verse 8.

*

Structurally the psalm could end here. But Francis adds a dismissal verse, in which the master of ceremonies/herald gives leave to the audience of the Hero's geste, reminding the listeners that they are now witnesses of what they have just heard. The disciples of the Lord-King must revive their awareness of the mission with which he has entrusted them: "As my Father has sent

Psalm 7

me, so do I send you" [Jn 20:21]; and "You will receive the power of the Holy Spirit descending on you and you will be my witnesses . . . even to the ends of the earth" [Acts 1:8]. Through this witnessing the whole earth will be moved:

9. **Let the whole earth be moved before his face; say among the nations: the Lord has reigned from the wood.**
   [Ps 95:9b–10a]

In fact, since the Hero's elevation on **the wood** of the cross and his glorification by the Father, he reigns over the **whole earth** (all of creation), which in him has found its rightful Lord, the **great King over all the earth** [v. 2]. By this victory of light over darkness, of truth over deceit and of life over death, this rightful **King** repairs the house of God, **zeal** for which **house has devoured** him [cf. PsF 5:9]. For Francis this same **zeal** should devour the disciples, so they, by their witnessing to the Hero's victory, may continue the mission of repairing God's house which, under the influence of the Prince of this world, had fallen into ruin.

The commissioning expression (**say among the nations**) must have struck a sensitive cord in Francis' experience of the gospel as Good News for it is this very instruction he left to his brothers in a letter that recaptures the content of PsF 7:8–9:

> Incline the ear of your heart and obey the voice of God's Son. Observe with your whole heart his mandates and carry out his counsels with a perfect mind. Acknowledge him because he is good and exalt him

COMMENTARY

in your works because the reason for which he sent you in the whole world is that by word and deed you may give witness to his voice and make known to all that there is no all-powerful one other than him [LtOrd 6–9].

*From Ascension to Advent
the following verses 10–12 are added.*

In the spirit of the liturgical feast of the Ascension, Francis begins by quoting the Creed, but with additions which insist on the Hero's sharing **the most holy Father**'s divine realm: the **heavens**, where, **seated at the right hand of the Father**, he is enthroned as **great King over all the earth** [PsF 7:2]:

10. **And he ascended to the heavens
and is seated at the right hand
of the most holy Father in heaven.**

At Vespers and Lauds of the Ascension, Francis would sing: "*Exalt* the King of kings and chant a psalm to God"; and at the third Nocturn of Matins: "He is greatly *exalted . . . above all the heavens. . . .*" This could have suggested the addition of Ps 56:12 as an amplification of the Ascension theme of PsF 7:10. Such an addition would have seemed all the more appropriate since the divine title, which the Hero had not regarded as "something to be grasped at" [Phil 2:6], he now received from the Father, who proclaimed him **God** [PsF 6:14b]. Moreover, the acclamation of Ps 56:12 is a fitting way for Francis to respond to the Hero's last words: **. . . I shall**

Psalm 7

be exalted among the nations and I shall be exalted on the earth [PsF 6:14b]:

> **11. Be exalted above the heavens, O God;
> and above all the earth your glory.**
> [Ps 56:12]

To end these Ascension verses, Francis could have once again quoted the Creed ("And he will come again to judge the living and the dead") as he had done for verse 10. Instead he preferred to revert to the text with which he had concluded PsF 6—most likely because of what this verse meant as the ultimate reversal of the Hero's unjust condemnation and death:

> **12. And we know that he comes;
> that he will come to judge justice.**
> [1Jn 5:7; Pss. 95:13b; 74:3]

***

As indicated in the rubric above, Francis would add these verses 10-12 throughout all of the period that extends from Ascension to Advent. He would do so most likely because of verses 11-12 which point to the expectation dimension of Advent [cf. PsF 13] and already announce the aspect which Francis highlights during this season: the Second Coming of the Hero in glory [cf. v. 11]. He will then judge the justice that had judged him. And the Father's saving plan, inaugurated by the Hero's geste will finally be brought to its fulfillment in the kingdom [cf. PsF 14].

THE SECOND SERIES
The Easter Variations

Liturgical Hour	Compline	Matins-Lauds	Prime	Terce	Sext	None	Vespers
PsF	8	9	3	9	9	9	7

For the Easter season Francis composed a new psalm, which is really a "new song" in the biblical sense. PsF **9** embodies the joy of the Hero's Easter victory. It is prayed not only at the hours of Matins-Lauds, but also at those of Terce, Sext and None. To open the series, Francis chose Ps 69 of the psalter, which became his psalm **8**; in it he found not only echoes of PsF 1 (Gethsemane), but also, as a secondary theme, an echo of the Easter victory.

These two new additions Francis combined with PsF 3 and 7 of the Passiontide series, which are also songs of victory, thus ensuring a definite triumphant stance to his celebration of this liturgical season.

Echoes of Gethsemane

For Compline
every day during Eastertime and the Christmas Season
and on Sundays and Major Feastdays
during Ordinary Time and during Lent

Introduction

For PsF 8 Francis took Ps 69 from the psalter without any changes. Ps 69 is usually divided into seven verses. Nevertheless, considering Francis' preference for the quatrain structure, one could be justified to make two verses out of the two complete sentences which make up verse 5. Moreover, as pointed out in the commentary leading to verse 5, this psalm is then composed of two quatrains, the first centered on the faith of those who oppose the Hero, the second centered on the Hero and on those who share his attitude toward the Father.

In this psalm of Francis one finds an echo of his first psalms of the geste regarding the Hero's first encoun-

PSALM 8

ters with opposition as well as an echo of the Hero's victory.

(Christ the Hero adresses the Father.)

Commentary

PsF 8 opens with the theme of the Hero's trust in the Father, which theme also concluded PsF 1, 2, 4, 5:

1. **God, see to my assistance;**
   Lord, make haste to help me.
   [Ps 69:1]

Verse 2 recalls to mind **the synagogue of the mighty** [PsF 2:9] who contrived to take the Hero's life:

2. **May they be confounded and shamed,**
   those who covet my soul.
   [Ps 69:2]

With verse 2 begins a series of similarly constructed requests: **May they. . . .** Moreover, verse 3 echoes the scene at Gethsemane [PsF 1:6] where the **enemies turn back** when they recognize the Hero as the accused they were sent to arrest:

3. **May they be repelled and blush with shame**
   those who wish me evil.
   [Ps 69:3]

The quatrain ends with a call for the shaming of those who gloat over their expected victory:

4. **May they retreat at once in shame,
   those who say to me: Good! Well done!**
   [Ps 69:4]

At first consideration, these requests do not seem to fit the Hero's attitude toward his enemies. But one can get a glimpse of how Francis may have read these verses by observing that the opening request (v. 2: **May they be confounded . . .**), which sets the tone for the following two, uses the very verb Francis chose in his *Salutation of Virtues* to express his view of the victory of good over evil:

> . . . each [virtue] **confounds** vices and sins.
> Holy Wisdom **confounds** Satan and all malice. . . .
> Holy Charity **confounds** every diabolical and
>   carnal temptation and all carnal fears.
> [SalVirt 8–9, 13]

With the verb "to confound" Francis suggests the idea of the virtues covering the vices with confusion, literally "shaming" them out of existence and taking their place.

Therefore, the requests of PsF 8:2–4, linked to a "shame-related" expression, do not speak the language of judgment and condemnation but rather that of a call to conversion. The enemies of the Hero had been blinded by Satan, the real Enemy. At the sight of the Father's glorification of the Hero, they are now invited to let evil be "shamed" out of their lives and become believers in his mission as the One sent by the Father. This illustrates how Francis tackled the problem of evil in the world.

*

Psalm 8

Thus far the psalm dwelt on the fate of those who were hostile to the Hero. The second quatrain opens with similarly constructed requests (**May they ...**) but these requests favor those who share the Hero's attitude toward the Father:

5. **May they exult and rejoice in you,
all who seek you.**
   [Ps 69:5a]

6. **And may they who love your salvation
always say:
May the Lord be magnified!**
   [Ps 69: 5b]

The last two verses echo the Hero's situation at the end of PsF 1 when, abandoned by all, he is taken prisoner and expresses his trust in the Father:

7. **But as for me, I am needy and poor;
O God, help me.**
   [Ps 69:6]

8. **You are my helper and my liberator,
Lord, do not delay.**
   [Ps 69:7]

In conclusion, even if taken entirely from the Psalter, Ps 69 proves to be a rather good choice as an echo or harmonic of the Hero's geste.

The New Song

*For Matins-Lauds
every day during Eastertime
and on Sundays and Major Feastdays during Ordinary Time
and during Lent*

*For Terce, Sext, None
during Eastertime*

Introduction

The Easter victory is God's "marvelous deed" par excellence which the exodus from Egypt foreshadowed. By leading the people through the Red Sea, God liberated them from the bondage of slavery to which Pharaoh had reduced them. In Christ the Hero's passage from this world to the Father, God liberates all peoples and indeed all of creation from the bondage of slavery in which the Prince of this world imprisoned them.

Psalm 9

PsF 9 is composed of two rather well-defined quatrains to which a third is added for the liturgical time of Ascension-Pentecost.

(Francis addresses the people.)

Commentary

At the time of the exodus from Egypt the people, led by Moses' sister Miriam, broke forth into a "new song" to celebrate this wonder. At their example the Church proclaims its song of joy, the *Exultet*. At Easter Francis, like a new Miriam, wants to lead all the peoples in a new song that would prolong that of the twenty-four Elders [Rev 5:9] evoked in the *Praises*:

1. **Sing to the Lord a new song
for he has done marvelous deeds.**
   [Ps 97:1a–b]

Then Francis chooses a text which parallels PsF 7:3 (by his beloved Son, God **brought about salvation in the center of the earth**). As the commentary on PsF 7:3 indicated, in that text Francis was referring to the legend of the cross planted **in the center of the earth**, on the very spot where Adam had been buried. Likewise the legend held that this was also the site where Abraham had built the altar on which to sacrifice his son Isaac, which sacrifice is recounted in the third reading of the Paschal Vigil. But this offering of old was only a sign of the Easter reality in which the heavenly

Father gave up his only Son [cf. Rom 8:32]. And as deacon, Francis would have sung in the *Exultet*, the opening proclamation of the Easter festivities:

> O inestimable goodness of love
> to redeem the servant [the Father] gave up
>   the Son!

This liturgical setting can help one enter into Francis' understanding of verse 2 of his Easter psalm:

> 2. **His right hand and his holy arm
>   have sacrificed his beloved Son.** [Ps 97:1c–d]

Interpreting the action of Abraham, "our father in faith," the author of the letter to the Hebrews writes [11:17,19] that: "Abraham . . . was offering his only son, . . . reasoning that God was able to raise from the dead; and he received Isaac back as a symbol" of the death-resurrection of the only Son, the **salvation made known** to all:

> 3. **The Lord has made known his salvation;
>   in the sight of the nations
>   he has revealed his justice.** [Ps 97:2]

Planted outside of the city, the sacrificial cross was, in effect, placed **in the sight of the nations** since many people had come from everywhere for the feast:

> Parthian, Medes, and Elamites, inhabitants of Mesopotamia, Judea and Cappadocia, Pontus and Asia, Phyrgia and Pamphylia, Egypt and the districts of Libya near Cyrene, as well as people from Rome, both Jews and proselytes, Cretans and Arabs [Acts 2:9–11].

Psalm 9

And all heard the proclamation of the **marvelous deeds** of God [PsF 9:1]. And all could, therefore, receive the revelation of God's **justice** [PsF 9:3], namely the resurrection and glorification of the One who had been sent:

> Jesus the Nazarene was a man commended to you by God with mighty deeds, wonders, and signs, which God worked through him in your midst, as you yourselves know. This man, delivered up by the set plan and foreknowledge of God, you put to death by the hand of evildoers. But God raised him up . . . [Acts 2:22–24].

Easter is **the day** of God's justice, of which the prophets had spoken. This divine **justice** is, in fact, the manifestation of God's **mercy**:

> **4. On that day the Lord sent his mercy and at night his song.** [Ps 41:9a–b]

Thus Francis concludes the first quatrain of his Easter song by returning to the idea of the **new song** proclaimed on Easter night. This first section focuses upon the event: God's love and mercy as manifested in the giving up of the only Son.

*

The second quatrain expresses a reaction of recognition and joy and is linked to the first by the bridge-word **day** (verse 4: **On that day** / verse 5: **This is the day**). Moreover, this second quatrain is well rooted in the Easter liturgy since it begins with a text which serves as antiphon for all the hours of the Office of Easter day and during the entire octave:

COMMENTARY

5. **This is the day the Lord has made;
   let us exult and be glad in it.**
   [Ps 117:24]

When he had arrived in Jerusalem, the Hero had been joyfully acclaimed by the crowd which had come for the feast:

> They took palm branches and went out to meet him, and cried out: "Hosanna! **Blessed is the one who comes in the name of the Lord,** the king of Israel! [Jn 12:13].

Now Francis calls all of creation to repeat this acclamation of its King because **the Lord is God,** and the Light who, like the symbolic Paschal candle and its forerunner the pillar of fire [Ex 13:21–22], guides all towards the new heaven and the new earth:

6. **Blessed is the one who comes
     in the name of the Lord;
   the Lord is God, and has shone upon us.**
   [Ps 117:26a, 27a]

7. **Let heavens rejoice and earth exult,
   let the sea and all that is in it be moved,
   let fields and all that is in them be glad.**
   [Ps 95:11–12a]

And may all the nations acclaim the new King:

8. **Bring to the Lord, families of nations,
   bring to the Lord glory and honor,
   bring to the Lord the glory due his name.**
   [Ps 95:7–8a]

*

Psalm 9

The following four verses are added:
- *on weekdays from the Ascension to the Octave of Pentecost;*
- *on Sundays and major feast days from Ascension to Advent and from the Octave of Epiphany to Holy Thursday.*

For the liturgical season extending from the Ascension to the octave of Pentecost, Francis assembled a third quatrain whose two first verses are linked to the Ascension. After having accomplished his mission, the Hero who had come to "dwell among us" [Jn 1:14], ascended into heaven whence he had come, and resumed his "equality with God" [Phil 2:6]:

9. **Kingdoms of the earth sing to God, chant a psalm to the Lord.**
    [Ps 67:33a]

10. **Chant a psalm to God who ascended to the East above the heaven of heavens.**
    [Ps 67:33b–34a]

But before his actual departure, the Hero had promised his disciples that they would "receive the **power** of the Holy Spirit who will descend on them" [Acts 1:8]. And it came to pass:

> when the time of Pentecost was fulfilled, they were all in one place together. And suddenly there came from heaven a sound like a strong burst of wind, and it filled the entire house where they were gathered. Then there appeared to them tongues as of fire, which parted and came to rest on each one of

them. And they were all filled with the Holy Spirit and began to speak in different tongues, as the Holy Spirit gave them to proclaim [Acts 2:1–4].

Francis mirrors this in the next verse of his psalm:

**11. Behold, he will give to his voice
the voice of power;
give glory to God over Israel,
his magnificence and his power
in the clouds.**
[Ps 67:34b–35]

And so began the Church, the community of his disciples! Henceforth the Hero's victory becomes, through the gift of the Holy Spirit, that of his disciples. They now share in the Spirit's **power**, which through them combats the powers of this world [cf. 1 Co 2:8]:

**12. God, wonderful in his saints,
the God of Israel himself
will give power and strength to his people;
Blessed be God!**
[Ps 67:36]

***

This PsF 9 is prayed not only at Matins-Lauds, but also at the hours of Terce, Sext and None where it prolongs the atmosphere of joy and acclamation of the new King which permeates the Easter season. Most likely for a similar reason, Francis would add the third quatrain also on Sundays and major feast days during Ordinary Time (after Pentecost and after Epiphany) and during Lent.

THE THIRD SERIES
The Sunday Variations

Liturgical Hour	Compline	Matins-Lauds	Prime	Terce	Sext	None	Vespers
PsF	8	9	3	10	11	12	7

Interestingly, the liturgical view of Sundays as the weekly celebration of the Paschal victory did not escape Francis' attention. For this he made use of four predominantly celebratory texts already used in the first and second series: PsF 3, 7, 8 and 9, to which he added three new psalms: PsF **10**, **11** and **12**. While PsF **10** echoes the joy of victory, PsF **11** and **12** stand out as harmonics of the corresponding psalms of Francis of the first series, namely, PsF 5 (the Hero's reflection as he hangs on the cross) and PsF 6 (the Hero facing death). Francis' Sunday variations prolong the jubilant mood of Easter during the entire the liturgical year, but with a reminder of the demanding road which leads to Paschal victory.

According to the rubrics which accompany Francis' texts, he prayed this series on Sundays throughout the year except during the Easter and Advent seasons when, even on Sundays, he would pray the psalms foreseen for those seasons.

Commentary

In accordance with the common liturgical practice, Francis prayed this new series also on major feast days. Note that the scribe who composed the rubrics reminds the reader to consider Holy Thursday as a major feast day "since it is the Lord's Passover."

A Shout of Joy

*For Terce
every day during Advent
and on Sundays and Major Feastdays
during Ordinary Time and during Lent*

Introduction

This psalm is structured on the basis of three calls addressed to the nations and tribes of the earth:

- **Raise to the Lord a shout of joy** . . .   [v. 1]
- **Come, listen** . . .   [v. 4]
- **Bless our God** . . .   [v. 7]

The following chart of the three sections introduced by these calls gives evidence of the prominent place occupied by Ps 65, which Francis may have first used here in its entirety:

Commentary

Section 1	Section 2	Section 3
v. 1 – Ps 65:1–2	v. 4 – Ps 65:16	v. 7 – Ps 65:8
v. 2 – Ps 65:3	v. 5 – Ps 65:17	v. 8 – Ps 71:17c–d
v. 3 – Ps 65:4	v. 6 – Ps 17:7c–d	v. 9 – Ps 71:18;135:4
		v. 10 – Ps 71:19.

It is obvious that Francis made very conscious choices for the present structure of PsF 10. In the verses of Ps 65, which begin each section of PsF 10, he did not maintain the order in which they occur in Ps 65.

It is also interesting to note that the opening verses of each section are all found in masses for Sundays for which Francis composed his psalm :

- v. 1–2: Third Sunday after Easter, introductory antiphon and verse;
- v. 4: Second Sunday after Epiphany and fourth Sunday after Pentecost, offertory verse;
- v. 7: Fourth Sunday after Easter, offertory verse.

One can also discern in PsF 10 an echo of Pentecost, especially since the gift of the Spirit was traditionally associated with the hour of Terce [cf. Acts 2:15] for which this psalm is chosen.

As was the case for PsF 7 and 9 which are also structured around invitations to praise God, it would be mostly Francis' voice one hears in PsF 10. This is quite evident in the first and third sections. As for the second section, which echoes the Hero's crying out to the Father [cf. PsF 1, 2, 4, 5], it would seem that Francis saw it as the voice of Christ. But it cannot be ruled out that he could have meant these three verses to be the disciple's witness to God's action in his own life.

As it stands PsF 10 has the appearance of an unfinished text. The major building blocks are in place, but the refinement of the text, so visible in the psalms of the geste, had not yet happened for PsF 10 by the time Francis died. This observation applies also to PsF 11 and 12.

Commentary

(Francis to the people—to the whole earth.)

The opening verse sets the tone for the psalm, namely, that of joy and praise. Francis has here replaced the word "God" by that of **Lord**, underlining the fact that he is referring to Christ the Hero:

1. **All the earth, raise to the Lord
   a shout of joy,
   chant a psalm to his name;
   give glory to his praise.**
   [Ps 65:1–2]

The **name** in whose honor **all the earth** is invited to sing is the name the Hero received after his victory, "the name which is above all names" [Phil 2:9], just as his divine being is above all others and worthy **to receive praise, glory, honor** . . . *[Praises 2]*.

The **Lord**-Hero is, therefore, the **God** who, with the Father and the Holy Spirit, accomplishes awesome deeds which confound his enemies of yesterday. They must now admit to their inaccurate utterances against him:

> 2. **Say to God:**
> **"How awesome are your deeds, O Lord;**
> **in the vastness of your strength**
> **your enemies shall be convinced**
> **of having lied about you.**
> [Ps 65:3]

As the enemies are **confounded** and, hopefully converted, **all the earth** rejoices at the sight of his works:

> 3. **May all the earth adore you**
> **and sing psalms to you;**
> **may it chant a psalm to your name."**
> [Ps 65:4]

*

(Christ the Hero addresses the crowd.)

In PsF 3:10 the Hero announces: **I will confess you among the nations. . . .** Verse 4 fulfills this promise and can be interpreted as an echo of Pentecost, since the sending forth by Christ of the disciples as witnesses "even to the ends of the earth" is linked to the gift of the Spirit [Ac 1:8]:

> 4. **Come, listen, all you who fear God,**
> **and I will recount**
> **how much he has done for my soul.**
> [Ps 65:16]

Verses 5 and 6 recall the Hero's constant prayer to the Father, who **heard his voice**. As mentioned above, this

Psalm 10

can also apply to Francis himself as disciple and witness:

5. **To him I cried out with my mouth
   and exulted with my tongue.**
   [Ps 65:17]

6. **And from his holy temple
      he heardmy voice
   and my crying out in his sight.**
   [Ps 17:7c–d]

*

(Francis to the people—to the whole earth.)

The quatrain that ends the psalm is a call to praise the Hero who, like Abraham, accepted being led by the will of the Father [PsF 6:12] and becoming a source of blessing for all the nations:

7. **Bless our God, you peoples,
   and make the voice of his praise be heard.**
   [Ps 65:8]

8. **And all the tribes of the earth
      shall be blessed in him,
   and all the peoples shall magnify him.**
   [Ps 71:17c–d]

The Hero had concluded his geste by prophesizing: **I will be exalted among the nations, and I will be exalted above all the earth** [PsF 6:15]. Then Francis acclaimed him with the phrase: **Blessed be the Lord,**

God of Israel . . . [PsF 6:15], an echo of which reverberates in the last two verses of PsF 10:

9. **Blessed be the Lord, the God of Israel
   who alone does great marvels.**
   [Ps 71:18; 135:4]

Finally, all of PsF 10 can be interpreted as an expression of Francis' desire to see the Hero's prophecy realized:

10. **And blessed be forever the name
     of his majesty,
     and may all the earth be filled
     with his majesty.
     So be it! So be it!**
     [Ps 71:19]

Thus the psalm ends with what seems to be a refrain, within which bursts forth the magnificent image of the Hero-King's majesty filling the whole earth, ushering in the new heavens and the new earth [Rv 21:1].

A Cry of Hope

For Sext
every day during Advent
and on Sundays and Major Feastdays
during Ordinary Time and during Lent

Introduction

This psalm of Francis is predominantly taken from Ps 19 and is completed with verses taken from three other psalms. It is composed of three unequal sections :

- 4 opening verses which express wishes (**May . . .**);
- 2 final verses [8–9] make up a refrain, which is also found in PsF 12;
- 3 verses [5–7] of the middle section.

Francis assembled this psalm for the Hour of Sext. In the geste this is the hour at which the Hero, fixed to the cross, reminds himself of the reasons he is in this situation [PsF 5].

313

Ps 19 was traditionally interpreted as the voice of the Church addressing Christ, so one can conclude in PsF 11 one hears the voice of Francis addressing his Hero. Moreover, one can easily recognize in the first section an overtone of compassion.

As in the case of PsF 10, PsF 11 presents itself as an unfinished work of Francis.

(Francis addresses the Hero and then the people [6b, 7a, 8–9].)

Commentary

As he hung on the cross, the Hero called out to the Father:

> **With my voice I cried out to the Lord. . . .**
> **I pour out my prayer in his sight,**
> **and I voice my trouble before him. . . .**
> **Escape has slipped away from me . . .**
>   [PsF 5:1,2,6].

And he concluded his prayer:

> **You are my most holy Father. . . .**
> **Make haste to help me,**
> **Lord, God of my salvation!**
>   [PsF 5:15–16].

The opening verses of PsF 11 follow a similar sequence regarding content:

> 1. **May the Lord hear you**
>   **on the day of tribulation;**

Psalm 11

**may the name of the God of Jacob
protect you.**
[Ps 19:2]

2. **May he send you help from the holy place,
and from Zion may he care for you.**
[Ps 19:3]

In PsF 5 the Hero had, in the final analysis, proclaimed love for the Father (PsF 5:9: **zeal for your house has devoured me**) and for humanity (PsF 5:7: **It is for you...**) as the motivating factor of his pursuit of his mission to the very end. He would be completely consumed by love just as a holocaust is completely consumed by fire:

3. **May he be mindful of your entire sacrifice,
and your holocaust be agreeable.**
[Ps 19:4]

The Hero had been sent to proclaim the Kingdom of God, which was to be sought after as the greatest treasure for which one could yearn. And he reminded his listeners that "where your heart is, there also is your treasure" [Mt 6:21]. Moreover, the Hero's exclusive life plan was to accomplish the will of the Father, as he expressed it in another of Francis' psalms:

**Holy Father, you have held my right hand
and according to your will you have led me
and you have lifted me up with glory.
For what is there in heaven for me,
and besides you, what have I wanted on earth?**
[PsF 6:12–13].

COMMENTARY

It is these thoughts that Francis seems to echo in the following verse:

4. **May he grant you what your heart desires,
   and may he keep firm your every plan.**
   [Ps 19:5]

Since the wishes expressed in the first section of this psalm are formulated with the knowledge of the outcome of the Hero's **tribulation**, they therefore become for Francis expressions of compassion for his Hero. These wishes also express his expectation for the continuation of the Hero's mission by his disciples.

*

Francis' hope for this continuation of the Hero's mission by his disciples is unflinching, because the Hero himself prayed to the Father for his disciples, as Francis recalled in his *Second Letter to the Faithful*:

> Oh how holy and how loving, pleasing, humble, peaceful, sweet, lovable and desirable above all things to have such a brother and son, who laid down his soul for his sheep and prayed to the Father saying: Holy Father, keep in your name those whom you have given me. . . . Father, all those whom you gave me in the world were yours and you have given them to me. . . . Bless and sanctify them. . . . and I want, Father, that where I am they also may be with me so that they may see my glory in your Kingdom [2LtF 56–60].

This conviction finds an appropriate expression in the opening verse of the second section of PsF 11:

Psalm 11

5. **We will rejoice in your salvation,**
   and in the name of our God
   we will be exalted.
   [Ps 19:6]

The vision of the disciples ultimately sharing in the exaltation of the Hero seems to motivate Francis's choice for the first part of verse 6:

6. **May the Lord fulfill all of your requests.**
   [Ps 19:7a–b]

The passage quoted above from Francis' *Second Letter to the Faithful* also includes the following:

> The Words which you gave me I have given to them; and they have accepted them and have truly *known* that I came from you and they have believed that *you have sent me* [2LtF 58].

This text could have inspired Francis to combine Ps 19:7c (**Now I have known that the Lord** made safe his **Christ**) with that of Ps 9:9b (**and he will judge the peoples with justice**) together with the expression (**sent his Son**) taken possibly from Jn 3:7, to compose the second half of verse 6:

Now I have known that the Lord sent
   Jesus Christ his Son,
and he will judge the peoples with justice.
[Ps 19:7c–d; 9:9b; Jn 3:7]

One can sense in this text Francis' enthusiastic assurance that the Hero's **requests** shall indeed be **fulfilled**. It is formulated as a confession of faith and sums up the Hero's mission which began with the Father send-

COMMENTARY

ing him, and will find completion with his coming in glory "to judge the living and the dead." And he will judge **with justice**, unlike those who judged him.

This awkward switch in verse 6 from a wish (**May the Lord . . .**) to an affirmation (**Now I have known . . .**) illustrates the fact that the text of PsF 11 remains an unfinished work of Francis.

In verses 1–6 the titles **Lord** and **God** designate the Father. In the following verses these titles are transferred to Christ, the victorious Hero of Francis' psalms.

At the beginning of his *Second Letter to the Faithful*, Francis writes of "the Word of the Father, so worthy, so holy and glorious" who received "in the womb of the holy and glorious Virgin Mary . . . the flesh of our humanity and frailty," and who, "though he was rich beyond all, willed to choose *poverty*" [2LtF 4–5]. For his sake Francis also chose the way of poverty. And as his first biographer reminds us, "the psalms which he sang with the most joy and love where those which magnified poverty" [2C 70]. The following verse would, therefore, carry great significance for him:

7. **And the Lord has become
   a refuge for the poor,
   a helper in times of tribulation;
   and may they, who have come to know
   your name, hope in you.**
   [Ps 9:10–11a]

Francis would most likely have read the **name** mentioned in this verse as the one the Hero received at his

Psalm 11

glorification: "the **name** which is above all names," that of **Lord** of all [Phil 2:9].

*

Francis had ended his psalm 10 with the exclamations:

> **Blessed be the Lord, God of Israel. . . .**
> **And blessed be forever the name of his**
>   **majesty. . . .**

In the final verses of PsF 11 and 12, which begin with the same words, Francis acknowledges that the Hero, **Lord God of Israel**, has become *his* God and that he has experienced this **God** to be his **protector** and **refuge**, his **helper** and **mercy**:

> 8. **Blessed be the Lord my God,**
>   **because he has become**
>   **my protector and my refuge**
>   **in the day of my tribulation.**
>   [Ps 143:1b; 58:17c–d]
>
> 9. **O my helper, I will sing to you,**
>   **for you, O God, [are] my protector,**
>   **my God, my mercy!**
>   [Ps 58:18]

***

This fervent acknowledgement by Francis of who the Hero is for him reawakens in him, every Sunday and on major feast days for which he composed the PsF 10, 11 and 12, the atmosphere of joy and acclamation of the new King which, as already noted in the commentary of PsF 9, permeates all of the Easter season.

COMMENTARY

A Child's Prayer

For None
every day during Advent
and on Sundays and Major Feastdays
during Ordinary Time and during Lent

Introduction

PsF 12 has a structure common to many of Francis' psalms, namely, two quatrains introduced by similar expressions (verse 1: **In you ... I have hoped** / verse 5: **In you I have been fortified**) and completed by a two-verse refrain [9–10]. It was composed for the Hour of None, the hour in the geste when the Hero is locked in the final hand-to-hand combat with the Prince of this world, the hour of his ultimate passage from this world to the Father [PsF 6].

Because of the many thematic links of PsF 12 with PsF 6, one is led to conclude that the voice heard in PsF 12

Psalm 12

is that of the Hero. Whereas the recollection of events of the Hero's last moments constituted an important part of PsF 6, PsF 12 speaks more directly to his inner sufferings and the spiritual trial involved.

(Christ the Hero addresses the Father.)

Commentary

This psalm could have been inspired by the great traditional victory hymn, the *Te Deum*, whose last verse taken from Ps 70:1 becomes the opening verse of PsF 12. The affirmations of this verse set the tone for the entire composition, namely, that the Hero's **hope** in the Father will not let him **be confounded forever**. Even if in his present situation on the cross he is put to shame (**confounded**), he knows that the outcome is in the Father's hands and can only be one which opens up to life. This certainty becomes the basis of the Hero's petitions:

1. **In you, O Lord, I have hoped,
let me not be confounded forever;
in your justice liberate me and rescue me.**
   [Ps 70:1b–2a]

2. **Incline your ear to me
and save me.**
   [Ps 70:2b]

3. **Be for me a protector-God
and a fortress,
so that you may make me safe.**
   [Ps 70:3a–b]

COMMENTARY

Verse 4 echoes the joy of verse 1 and, together with it, functions as a book-end which encloses and injects hope into the Hero's inner sufferings as expressed in verses 2–3:

4. **For you are my patience, O Lord,**
   my hope, O Lord, from my youth.
   [Ps 70:5]

Hope and **patience** are two of the names of the Father, which also appear in Francis' *Praises of God*.

*

The second quatrain expands on the theme of the Hero's origins already present in verse 4 (**from my youth**). This quatrain weaves the past as the basis of confidence and **hope** in the present situation with the joy and praise which come from the Hero's anticipated victory:

5. **In you I have been fortified from the womb,**
   from my birth you are my protector;
   of you my song will always be.
   [Ps 70:6]

Verse 5 contains a discrete suggestion of the Hero's mother (**from the womb, from my birth**). She had first appeared in the **night** in PsF 2:3–4 as a soft "lunar" light when the bright daylight of the Father had all but disappeared. Here, as in PsF 6, she is discreetly present at the foot of the cross when "darkness came over the whole land" [Lk 23:44]. And as PsF 15 will evoke the **night** of the Hero's birth at Bethlehem, PsF 12 recalls

Psalm 12

his new birth, his passage from this world to that of the Father, a vision of joy:

> 6. **May my mouth be filled with praise**
> **that I may sing your glory,**
> **all the day long, your greatness.**
> [Ps 70:8]

In his teachings the Hero had referred to the joy that replaces the pangs of pain endured by the woman giving birth to her child [Jn 16:21]. Now is the time of labor and new birth for the Hero. It is the **night** of **anguish** when he cried out: "My God, My God, why have you abandoned me?" [Mt 27:46]. To recreate this dramatic moment, Francis resorted to a poignant expression (**turn not your face away from your child**) and a sense of urgency (**answer me quickly**):

> 7. **Answer me, O Lord, for kind is your mercy;**
> **in the greatness of your mercies look**
> **upon me.**
> [Ps 68:17]
>
> 8. **And turn not your face away**
> **from your child;**
> **answer me quickly for I am in anguish.**
> [Ps 68:18]

*

However dark the **night** of **tribulation** may be, the Hero does not doubt the Father's saving presence. Beyond the darkness of Golgotha the dawn of victory and new life bursts forth:

> 9. **Blessed be the Lord my God,**
> **because he has become my protector and**
> **my refuge**
> **in the day of my tribulation.**
> [Ps 143:1b; 58:17c–d]
>
> 10. **O my helper, I will sing to you,**
> **for you, O God, [are] my protector,**
> **my God, my mercy!**
> [Ps 58:18]

THE FOURTH SERIES
The Advent Motif

Liturgical Hour	Compline	Matins-Lauds	Prime	Terce	Sext	None	Vespers
PsF	13	14	3	10	11	12	7

For the Advent season Francis put together a series of texts which mirrors the balanced recollection of the Paschal mystery found in the Sunday series, but with the addition of a new motif, namely, the expectation (PsF **13**) and the vision of the fulfillment (PsF **14**) of the Hero's victory in the Kingdom of the Father. What is emphasized here is the preparation not of the Hero's historical birth, but of his Second Coming in glory to bring to completion God's plan for creation.

A Time of Expectation

*For Compline
every day during Advent*

Introduction

Francis took PsF 13 directly from the psalter without editing. With the repetition of the expression **How long . . .** , the first verses of this psalm fittingly espouse the spirit of Advent as a time of expectation and anticipation.

In line with Francis' preference for quatrains, PsF 13 can be divided into two sections consisting of four and two verses. As will be noted in the commentary, verse 5 contains a transition which can validate this suggested structure.

Because of its links to Gethsemane [cf. PsF 1] the voice here is most likely that of the Hero.

(Christ the Hero addresses the Father.)

Psalm 13

Commentary

In verse 1 of this psalm, one can hear echoes of Gethsemane as evoked in PsF 1:5,9 (**be not far from me . . . do not keep your aid far from me**), but with overtones of the last temptation, the temptation of despair [cf. PsF 5:9b–14]. This is especially so in the sense of urgency created by the recurring expression **How long**:

1. **How long, O Lord, will you forget me in the end?**
   How long will you turn your face from me?
   [Ps 12:1]

Verse 2 brings to mind the image of a person twisting and turning all night long, besieged by conflicting thoughts, and carrying the burden of a heavy heart all day long:

2. **How long shall I consider ideas in my soul, pain in my heart all through the day?**
   [Ps 12:2]

At Gethsemane the **enemy** had taken the upper hand by having the Hero arrested. The subsequent events had seemingly confirmed the **enemy**'s advantage over the Hero:

3. **How long will my enemy be exalted over me?**
   Look and hear me, O Lord, my God.
   [Ps 12:3–4a]

Commentary

But a breech opened in the wall of anguish which had closed in on the Hero. The Father was neither blind nor deaf to his situation (**Look and hear**). As long as the Father's light shone on him, the Hero would not be engulfed in the darkness of **death**; and **the enemy**, the Prince of this world, would not **prevail against him**:

> 4. **Enlighten my eyes**
>   **that I may not sleep in death,**
>   **that my enemy may never say:**
>   **"I prevailed against him."**
>   [Ps 12:4b–5a]

Two equivalencies are hinted at here:

- despair = night (darkness) = death;
- hope = light = life.

Had the Hero succumbed to the temptation of despair [cf. PsF 5:10–14], he already would have been spiritually in the grips of **death**. But the Hero foiled the **enemy**'s attack by calling upon the **light**, and consequently, upon the life which comes from God.

Furthermore, one can notice how the theme of **sleep** links this psalm to Gethsemani [PsF 1]. Before his arrest in the garden, the Hero had asked his disciples to "stay awake" with him. Returning to them after having prayed to the Father and finding them asleep, "he said to Peter: So you could not stay awake with me for an hour? Be on your guard and pray that you may not enter into temptation" [Mt 26:40–41]. And once again finding them asleep, he chided them: "Sleep on now and rest! Behold, the hour has come and the Son of

Psalm 13

Man is to be betrayed into the hands of sinners" [Mt 26:45].

Interestingly enough, the same theme of **sleep** situates PsF 13 in the Advent season. Shortly before his arrest, while speaking of his return in glory, the Hero had admonished his disciples to "stay awake" since no one knows the day of his coming [cf. Mt 25:13]. Thus Francis would have read in Ps 12, which he had adopted as his psalm 13, a reminder of Advent as a time of expectation and of anticipation. A reminder also that, as the wise virgins of the parable [cf. Mt 25:1ff], the Hero's disciples should remain in a state of alertness so as to be able to greet him with burning lamps when he returns as the bridegroom to inaugurate the eternal wedding feast of the Kingdom.

*

In PsF 1, the psalm linked to Gethsemane, after having recalled the enemies' maneuvers against him, the Hero concluded: **But I prayed. . . .** In PsF 13:4 there is a similar movement. After having noted that the enemies **would rejoice if** he **became troubled**, he adds: **but I hoped in your mercy**. This supplies the inner transition from the possibility of despair to the assurance of the Father's presence:

5. **Those who torment me would rejoice
    if I became troubled;
    but I hoped in your mercy.**
    [Ps 12:5b–6a]

Commentary

This assurance of God's **mercy** opens on the joyful and praise-filled anticipation of his **salvation**:

6. **My heart shall exult in your salvation;
   I will sing to the Lord
     who granted good things to me,
   and I will sing to the name of the Lord,
     Most High.**
   [Ps 12:6b–d]

In his *Earlier Rule* Francis wrote: ". . . let us give back all *good things* to the Most High and Supreme Lord God, and acknowledge that all *good things* are God's, and for all things thank God, from whom all *good things* come" [17:17]. Francis, therefore, would have found it very fitting that PsF 13 would end on this thought: **I will sing to the Lord who granted good things to me**.

A Vision of Fulfillment

*For Matins-Lauds
every day during Advent*

Introduction

The ten verses of PsF 14 are the result of two very different procedures of composition. Whereas the first four verses are constructed from material taken from many sources, the last six all come from a single source, Ps 68. Furthermore, this last section can be divided into two sub-sections, each beginning with an invitation:

- verse 5: **Let the poor see and rejoice. . . .**
- verse 7: **Let the heavens and earth praise him. . . .**

These different elements reveal that PsF 14 is composed of two quatrains [vss. 1–4; 7–10] separated by a pivotal two-verse section [vss. 5–6].

Parallels with other psalms of Francis in which Christ the Hero is clearly the speaker, suggest that his voice is also the one heard in the first quatrain of PsF 14. But with verse 5 begins a text of another tone more in line with Francis' voice.

Commentary

(Christ the Hero addresses the Father.)

For the opening verse of PsF 14 Francis brought together three biblical texts which all begin with the same words (**I will confess you**). With this phrase the Hero acknowledges the Father's role in the mission with which he has been entrusted:

- Is 12:1 **I will confess you, Lord**, for you were angry with me;
  your rage has been changed and **you have consoled me.**
  Behold, **God my savior** . . . [cf PsF 14:2].
- Sir 51:1 **I will confess you, Lord, King**, and I will praise you,
  God, my Savior [cf. PsF 14:2].
- Mt 11:25 **I will confess you, Father, Lord of heaven and earth** for you have hidden these things from the wise and the prudent and have revealed them to little ones.

Francis most likely took his opening cue from the last of these three texts, Mt 11:25, which then sets the tone for all of PsF 14. Even the mention of the "little ones"— in opposition to the "wise and prudent"—**announces**

Psalm 14

the poor of verses 5 and 6 who inherit the kingdom [cf vv. 9–10], since entrance to the kingdom supposes a conversion to the receptivity of "little ones" [Mt 18:3].

One notices that Francis excluded from his use of Is 12:1 the passage which speaks of God's anger ("you were angry . . . ; your rage . . ."). This exclusion of images of divine anger or revenge characterizes all of Francis' psalms.

Francis retains the three titles attributed to God in his sources: **Lord**, **King**, and **Father**. To the title **Father** he adds the qualifier **most holy**, as he is often wont to do:

1. **I will confess you, Lord, most holy Father,**
   King of heaven and earth,
   for you have consoled me.
   [Is 12:1; Mt 11:25; Sir 51:1]

This opening verse serves as a bridge between Advent and Ordinary Time which begins after Pentecost and ends with Advent. Although Francis composed PsF 14 for the Advent season, he did not forget that the Second Coming of the Hero will climax this Ordinary Time, a time of witness (**I will confess you . . .**). The Ordinary Time of the liturgical year symbolizes the time of the Church when the Hero acts through his disciples.

This same verse in its conclusion (**you have consoled me**) could well have brought to Francis' mind two passages from the prophet Isaiah's "Book of Consolation," which would thus link the beginning of PsF 14 to the Advent season. The first passage was read during the fourth week of Advent, at Matins of Wednesday:

COMMENTARY

> Therefore the Lord shall *console* Zion
> And shall *console* all her ruins... [Is 51:3]

The second:

> *Be consoled, be consoled* my people... [Is 40:1]

which opens the "Book of Consolation," was proclaimed at Christmas during the second reading of Matins [Is 40: 1-8] and affirms that the "Consolation of Israel" [Lk 2:25] — object of the Advent expectation — is about to appear.

Verse 2 of PsF 14 continues with the text of Is 12, already present in verse 1, and picks up a theme — that of salvation — which frequently occurs in the liturgy of Advent:

> 2. **You are God, my Savior;**
>   **I will act confidently and will not be afraid.**
>   [Is 12:2a; Ps 24:5b]

Francis made a slight but significant change in the text of Is 12:2 which begins: *Behold,* **God** (is) **my Savior.** . . . To maintain the coherence of the Hero's addressing the Father, he changed the opening words to: **You are God, my Savior.** . . . This is a procedure similar to the one to which Francis already had recourse at the end of PsF 2 and 5 (**You are my Father** . . .).

For some reason, Francis did not continue in verse 3 the type of adaptation, words addressed to the Father, he had initiated in verse 2. In verse 3 he passes from Is 12 *(for* **my strength and my praise**) to Ex 15, the victory hymn sung by the Israelites after the destruction of Pharaoh's armies in the waters of the Red Sea:

Psalm 14

3. **My strength and my praise [is] the Lord
and he has become my salvation.**
   [Is 12:2b; Ex 15:2]

As for the Israelites of old, God became **strength** and **salvation** for the Hero and for the Hero's disciples. Moreover, the Israelites' crossing of the Red Sea had taken place in the **night** and they were assured of their deliverance as the first rays of morning light dispelled the darkness. The Hero's birth, the prelude to his saving geste, also took place at **night** [cf. PsF 15:5]. In turn this geste which began in the **night** [cf. PsF 1 and 2], would end with the Father giving the Hero victory over the **night** of death [cf. PsF 9:4] as darkness covered the earth [cf. Mt 27:45]. This backdrop, which contrasts

> **night**/darkness/death
> with
> **day**/light/life,

highlights an important dimension of PsF 14. For Francis composed PsF 14 to be prayed exclusively at the **night** Office of Advent, a time when the whole world awaits the final manifestation of the Hero as "light of the world" [Mt 25:6; Jn 8:12]. Thus, this manifestation—his Second Coming—will shatter forever the darkness as well as the consequent blindness, which characterized the reign of the Prince of this world [cf. PsF 2:9].

Verse 3 ended with the word **salvation**. To understand better what Francis would have read into this word **salvation**, one must keep in mind how he views God's major interventions in the history of the world. He does so in a dynamic tripartite sequence: creation—redemption—salvation, the last moment being projected into the future as the culmination of the other two. In chapter 23 of his *Earlier Rule* Francis proclaims that God, "our Creator, Redeemer and Savior" [v. 9] has "created us, redeemed us, and *will save* us by his mercy alone" [v. 8]. The beginning of that same chapter 23 first recalls how the Father had *created* all things

> "by his only Son with the Holy Spirit" [v. 1]

and how the Father had brought about his Son's birth and

> "willed to *redeem* us captives through his cross and blood and death" [v. 3].

Then Francis puts the **salvation** moment in parallel with the Hero's Second Coming:

> And we give you thanks because your Son himself *will come again* in the glory of his majesty. . .and say to those who have known, adored and served you in penance: Come, you, blessed of my Father, receive the kingdom which has been prepared for you from the beginning of the world [v. 4].

The *redemption* which, in the case of the Hero's humanity, has already reached its completion in **salvation**, can be sung about rightly with the words of the song of the exodus:

4. **Your right hand, O Lord,
    is magnificent in strength,**

Psalm 14

**your right hand, O Lord,
has struck the enemy;
and in the greatness of your glory
you deposed my adversaries.**
[Ex 15:6–7a]

In the common text this verse would end: **you deposed** *your* **adversaries**. But the same text in Francis' breviary, which is kept in the Poor Clare Protomonastery in Assisi, reads: **you deposed my adversaries**. And this reading served well Francis' purpose in the present case, since the Hero is here referring to the **adversaries** he encountered in the accomplishment of his mission.

With the Hero's victory, the **Enemy**, the Prince of this world, has been **struck** down. And those who, blinded by the **Enemy**'s lies (the "malices" spoken of in of *Salutation of the Virtues* 9), had become the Hero's **adversaries**, are now deposed from the position of power they had assumed over him. Already, when the angel Gabriel had announced to the Hero's Mother that she would give birth to him, she had recognized the Lord God's intervention and proclaimed that God would, among other things, "*depose* the mighty from the throne" [Lk 1:52].

In the days of old, the Almighty had opened for Moses and all "the children of Israel" [Ex 15:1] the road to the Promised Land of Canaan. Now the Father had opened for the Hero and for all "the children of God" [Jn 11:52] the road to the Promised Land of the kingdom.

*

COMMENTARY

(Francis addresses the people.)

At the head of this march of humanity towards the kingdom and immediately following Christ, the new Moses, are those who share in his initial and redeeming choice, which Francis expressed in the following manner :

> Though he was rich beyond all, in this world he himself, together with the most blessed Virgin, his Mother, willed to choose poverty. [2LtF 5]

Ps 68 furnished Francis with an appropriate image of the joy of those with whom the Hero had identified himself, "What you have done to the least. . ." [Mt 25:40]:

> 5. **Let the poor see and rejoice . . .**
>   [Ps 68:33a]

To illustrate which psalms Francis prayed with the most joy and love, that is those psalms which glorify poverty, Thomas of Celano quoted this very verse [cf. 2C 70]. In Francis' view, however, his Hero had chosen poverty not only to identify with the *materially* poor, victims of envy and greed who are called to rest "in the bosom of Abraham" [Lk 16:22], but also—and more importantly—to indicate the essential attitude which opens one's life to its fulfillment in the kingdom of heaven :

> Blessed the poor in spirit for theirs is the kingdom of heaven [Mt 5:3; Adm 13].

Francis had personally experienced the transition from material riches to poverty. And this helped him understand and practice the basic message of the beatitude

Psalm 14

of "the poor in spirit" and the profound significance of the Hero's teaching:

> Everyone of you who does not renounce all that you possess cannot be my disciple [Lk 14:33].

In the *Later Rule* Francis had spelled out for himself and for his brothers the practical consequences of this teaching:

> The brothers shall appropriate nothing for themselves, neither house, nor place nor anything else. And as pilgrims and strangers in this age, serving the Lord in poverty and humility, let them go confidently for alms; nor should they be ashamed because, the Lord made himself poor for us in this world. This is the eminence of that most high poverty which has established you, my most beloved brothers, heirs and kings of the kingdom of heaven. . . . May this be your *portion*, which leads into *the land of the living* [6:1–5].

This last sentence, without doubt, was inspired by Ps 141:6:

> I cried out to you, O Lord;
> I said: you are my hope,
> my *portion in the land of the living*.

Francis put the first five verses of Ps 141 on the lips of his Hero as he hung from his death-bed, the cross [cf. PsF 5:1ff]. Francis himself prayed this very same psalm as he lay on his death-bed [cf. 1C 109]. From this usage of Ps 141 in these two instances, one gets a significant insight into what Francis had in mind as he incorporated Ps 141:6 into the *Later Rule* 6: only one who, like

COMMENTARY

the Hero, accepts total dependence upon the Creator (and therefore essential poverty) can accept God as one's *portion* and can also then accept being led by the Hero into *"the land of the living."*

The injunction which opens chapter 6 of the *Later Rule*, as quoted above ("The brothers shall appropriate nothing to themselves . . ."), refers first to specific material things (houses, places), but then generalizes beyond all limits: "nor anything else." Such all-inclusiveness is based, in Francis' view, on the fact that creatures cannot, without blasphemy, usurp the place of the Creator and sole owner of all that exists:

> Let us refer every good to the Most High and Supreme Lord God and recognize that *every good is God's,* and let us refer all graces to [God] *from whom every good comes* [ER 17:17].

Francis seems to have given the widest possible scope to such New Testament texts as that of the First Letter of Peter:

> Whatever gift each of you may have received, use it in service to one another, like good dispensers of the grace of God in its many forms [1Pt 4:10].

Such a well-integrated recognition of total dependence on the Creator, coupled with a fraternal solidarity with the victims of jealousy, envy, greed and the thirst for power, [cf. PsF 7:8] presupposes that one's life is resolutely centered on the essentials, according to the Hero's teaching: "Seek first the kingdom of God and his justice and all the rest will be given to you as well" [Mt 6:33].

Psalm 14

This all-encompassing vision of "most high poverty. . .which leads into the land of the living" undergirds the second half of PsF 14:5:

> **. . . seek the Lord and your soul will live.**
> [Ps 68:33b]

Though the Hero had physically become the Enemy's captive, nevertheless he belonged to the Father who heard his confident call and gave him victory over the Enemy. The same outcome awaits all **the poor** who would follow the Hero's teachings and example and whom the Enemy would also consider his **captives**, but who in reality belong to the Father:

> 6. **For the Lord heard the poor,
> and has not despised his captives.**
> [Ps. 68:34]

One can understand why Thomas of Celano would underscore Francis' preference for psalm verses which insist on the fact that **the poor** will not be forgotten and that their patience will not be in vain [cf. Ps 9:19 and 2C 70; see also PsF 6:15].

*

Verse 7, which opens the last quatrain of PsF 14, springs from the assurance expressed in verse 6. It is a call to praise which involves all of creation destined to partake in "the liberty of the glory of the children of God" [Rm 8:20–22]:

> 7. **Let heaven and earth praise him,
> the sea and all that moves in them.**
> [Ps 68:35]

341

COMMENTARY

Like the Hero, those who by faith had put their security in God now experience the full reality of that security :

8. **For God will make secure Zion,**
   and the cities of Juda will be built up.
   [Ps 68:36a–b]

The mission the Hero had initiated in PsF 5:9 (**Holy Father, zeal for your house has devoured me . . .**), and for the continuation of which his disciple Francis had been called ("Francis, go and repair my house . . ."), will find its final completion when the "ancient world" [Rv 21:4] will be completely transformed into "a new heaven" and "a new earth" [Rv 21:1], as prophesized in the vision of John:

> I saw the holy city, the New Jerusalem, descending from heaven, from God . . . [Rv 21:2].

And there, in the holy city, will end the journey of all the children of God who, living as "pilgrims and strangers in this age," [LR 6:2] followed the Hero's lead. Their witness to the Hero's gospel, the Good News, constantly bore the brunt of the Prince of this world. But now this "murderer from the beginning" [Jn 8:44], is completely and permanently disarmed and "sent into the pool of fire and sulfur" [Rv 20:10]. His justice has been judged [cf. PsF 6:16] and his victims now inherit the kingdom which has been prepared for them "since the beginning of the world" [Mt 25:34]:

9. **And they** [= the poor] **will dwell there,**
   and will acquire it by inheritance.
   [Ps 68:36c]

Psalm 14

**10. And the descendants of his servants
will possess it
and those who love his name will live in it.**
[Ps 68:37]

The children of God, who had been dispersed by the cunning Enemy, are now gathered in unity [cf. Jn 11:52] in the completely restored "house of God" their Father. The verbs **dwell**, **possess** and **live**, in conjunction with the image of the bride associated with the New Jerusalem, open a window to the vision of an intimate dimension of the kingdom as fulfillment of the new and everlasting covenant sealed in the Hero's blood [cf. Lk 22:20], for:

> the New Jerusalem descends from heaven, beautiful as a bride adorned for her spouse. I heard a loud voice proclaiming . . . : Behold the dwelling of God with humanity! And he will **dwell** among them and this people shall be his, and the very God-with-them will be their God [Rev 21:2–3].

***

With this impressive vision of the fulfillment of the Father's plan for creation, Francis very fittingly ends this psalm composed for the Advent season during which the Christian liturgy evokes the Hero's final glorious manifestation and echoes creation's cry:

> Amen! Come, Lord Jesus!
> [Rv 22:20]

Feria sexta post pascha

Introduxit

uos dominus i terra;

fluentem lac et mel

alleluia et ut lex do

mini semper sit i ore

THE FIFTH SERIES
The Nativity Motif

Liturgical Hour	Compline	Matins-Lauds	Prime	Terce	Sext	None	Vespers
PsF	8	15	3	15	15	15	15

For the Christmas season, which held a very special place in his heart, Francis concentrated his efforts only on one text, PsF 15, and prayed it at every liturgical hour of the day except Compline and Prime. For these two hours he resorted to PsF 8 and 3 which foretell the difficulty of the mission with which the new-born Hero will be entrusted.

The carefully crafted text of PsF 15 modulates the three-fold motif of

- the Hero's divine origin and kingship,
- his humble, earthly beginnings,
- and his manifestation to the nations of the world

while all of creation expresses its joy.

The Hero's Origin and Birth

*For all the Hours
(except Compline and Prime)
every day during the Christmas Season*

Introduction

This is the last psalm of Francis' *Office of the Passion*. Since he had begun with the liturgical season of Passiontide, and not having arranged any special psalms for Lent, his Little Office ends with the liturgical season of Christmas. Considering the large amount and variety of texts used together with the well-defined structure of this psalm (4/4/4/1 verses), one can conclude that Francis reworked it extensively, most likely over a period of many years, and probably used it at various stages of its evolution as a point of departure for PsF 7 and 9.

(Francis addresses the people.)

Psalm 15

Commentary

The first biographies of Francis all note the very special place Christmas held in his vision of humanity's salvation in Christ. An anonymous author who could very well have been Brother Leo, one of Francis' most constant and faithful companions, explains:

> For Blessed Francis had greater reverence for the Lord's Nativity than for any other solemnity of the Lord because, as Blessed Francis said, although in all his other festivities the Lord brought about our salvation, nevertheless, from the very fact that he was born for us, it follows that we would be saved [AC 110].

This view of Christmas could have been suggested to Francis by the verse and response of the first Vespers of the Nativity:

- V/ Tomorrow the iniquity of the earth shall be erased.
- R/ And the Savior of the world shall reign over us.

It is, therefore, not surprising that his Christmas song would begin in an atmosphere of great joy and exultation:

1. **Exult in God our help,
   raise to the Lord God, living and true,
   a shout of joy with a voice of exultation.**
   [Ps 80:2a; 46:2; 1Th 1:9]

The cause and origin of this jubilation can be found only in **the Lord God**, that is the Triune God according

Commentary

to Francis' usual way of using this expression. Therefore, this exultation stems from who God is as well as from what God has done and continues to do. But at Christmas, most likely inspired by the Prologue of John's gospel, Francis' contemplation centers first on the kingship of his Hero:

2. **Because the Lord [is] the Most High,
the awesome, great King over all the earth.**
   [Ps 46:3]

It is noteworthy that the motif of the kingship of the Lord Jesus Christ is one of the important themes of the liturgical vigil of Christmas. The offertory of the mass proclaims: "He will enter the King of glory. . . ." In the Liturgy of the Hours, the following two antiphons are used repeatedly:

"The King of peace has been magnified over all
   the kings of the earth."
"You will see the King of kings coming from the
   right hand of the Father."

And this great **King** is the **beloved son**, the One sent by the **Father**:

3. **For the most holy Father of heaven,
   our King before all ages,
   sent his beloved Son from on high,
   and he was born of the Blessed Virgin
   Holy Mary.**
   [Ps 73:12; 143:7; Ga 4:4; Creed]

In his devotion to Mary, the Mother of his Hero, Francis always considers her in the role she assumes in the mystery of salvation. A passage from Celano proves to be particularly interesting concerning this Christmas psalm of Francis:

> [Francis] embraced with inexpressible love the Mother of Jesus since she made the Lord of majesty a brother for us [2C 198].

The Incarnation is therefore the first step towards the kingship which the Father will bestow upon the Hero:

> 4. **He called upon him: You are my Father,
> and he placed him as the firstborn,
> the highest above the kings of the earth.**
> [Ps 88:27a, 28]

When did the Hero thus **call upon** his **Father**? Throughout all of his Passion, his struggle with the Enemy:

- **Holy Father, do not keep your aid far from me....** [PsF 1: 9; 4:9]
- **You are my most holy Father... Make haste to help me....** [PsF 2:11–12; 5:15–16]
- **I will cry out to my most holy Father....** [PsF 3:3]

And the **Father** in reply received him **with glory.** [PsF 7:11]

It is to be noted that Francis makes two significant changes to the text he quotes in verse 4 taken from Ps 88:27a, 28, a text which often recurs in the Christmas liturgy:

> He *will call* upon *me*: You are my Father,
> and *I will place* him as the firstborn,
>   the highest above the kings of the earth.

COMMENTARY

The first change concerns the verbs which in Ps 88 are *in the future tense* because they referred at the time of their composition to a future reality. But in his PsF 15, Francis recalls *past* events: the Father **sent his beloved Son** and **he was born of the Blessed Virgin Holy Mary** [v. 3]. Therefore, Francis harmonizes verse 4 with the preceding verses of his psalm and puts the verbs in the past tense: **he called. . .he placed**. It is because of those past events, as well as others evoked in the other psalms of Francis, that the Hero is seen *today* as **the awesome, great King over all the earth** [v. 2]. For that reason Francis invites all to **exult** [v. 1].

Secondly, Francis changes the orientation of the dialogue. In the text of Ps 88 one hears the voice of God, therefore, the **Father** ("He will call upon me: You are my Father, and I will place him . . ."). But in PsF 15, it is the voice of the singer—Francis—which is heard. In fact, in all of the psalms of Francis, one never hears the voice of the **Father** because he "lives in inaccessible light" [Adm 1:5]. Moreover, for Francis the "voice" of the Father is his Incarnate Word.

This change in the text also gave Francis an occasion to apply a literary technique which he often uses, namely, designating by use of the same word, two realities whose equality he wants to affirm:

He *(ipse*: the Son) **called upon him** *(ipsum*: the Father). . .
and he *(ille*: the Father) **placed him** *(illum*: the Son). . . .

Psalm 15

The model for this rather unusual structure is most likely to be found in the opening verse of Ps 129 where the word *Lord* identifies both God and the one of whom the psalm sings:

> Ps 129:1 – The *Lord* said to my *Lord*. . . .
> PsF 15:4 – **He called upon him** . . .
> and *he* placed *him*. . . .

Francis prayed Ps 129 at Vespers on Sundays and on major feastdays. And the verse which is referred to here had been traditionally interpreted as the Father addressing the risen Christ.

For Francis this is, therefore, a way of inscribing in the very structure of the sentence (**He called upon him . . . and he placed him. . . .**) the fact that the Hero (the One sent), who is truly human (**born of . . . Mary**), is also truly divine like the Father (the Sender).

The first quatrain of PsF 15 concentrated not so much on the birth of the Hero as such, but rather situates this event in the wider context of his entire mission, at the end of which he receives royalty from the Father.

This vision of the Christ event which affirms the divine origin of Francis' Hero is akin to the view of the Evangelist John who, in the Prologue of his gospel, stresses the divine origin of the One who at Christmas came to dwell among us:

> In the beginning was the Word, and the Word was God. . . . And the Word became flesh and made his dwelling among us [Jn 1:1,14].

COMMENTARY

Francis echoes this in his *Second Letter to the Faithful* where he writes about "our Lord Jesus Christ, who is the Word of the Father":

> . . . this Word of the Father, so worthy, so holy and glorious, the most high Father sent from heaven into the womb of the holy and glorious Virgin Mary from whom he received the real flesh of our humanity and our frailty. Though he was rich beyond all other things . . . he willed to choose poverty [2LtF 4–6].

Francis' Hero, the man from Nazareth, [cf. Acts 2:22] is truly the Son of God, **born of the Blessed Virgin Holy Mary.**

*

The very first words of the second quatrain focus on Christmas as an historical event:

5. **On that day the Lord sent his mercy and at night his song.**
   [Ps 41:9a–b]

This verse contains the structure of the entire quatrain:

On that day	: v. 6	**This is the day**
the Lord sent his mercy	: v. 7	the . . . child was given to us
and at night his song	: v. 8	**Glory to God**

At the beginning of verse 5 Francis introduces an interesting change in the text of Ps 41:9. The quoted text says: "*By day* the Lord sent. . . ." Francis replaces the first words with **On that day**, thus focusing attention on the past event. He was most probably influenced

Psalm 15

here by an antiphon of the first Sunday of Advent: "*On that* day sweetness (honey) will be distilled from the mountains. . . ." At Matins of Christmas Francis would sing as response to the second reading: "*Today* throughout the earth the heavens became as honey. . . ."

Finally, verse 5 proclaims that it is **the Lord** (here the Father) who took the initiative: **The Lord sent.** . . . The Hero's birth is, therefore, God's great gift to humanity. As Brother Leo, Francis' faithful companion, recalls in the text quoted above [cf. AC 110], Francis saw the Hero's birth as the dawn of a new era, an era of hope. Christmas was therefore for Francis a very special day, a day of great joy, a day of exultation and sharing, just as the Father **on that day** had shared with us the precious gift of the Savior. Thus, to the already-cited text of the *Assisi Compilation* [110], Brother Leo adds:

> For that reason he wanted that on such a day every Christian exult in the Lord, and for love of him who gave himself to us, everyone should joyfully be generous, not only to the poor but also to the animals and birds.

In verse 5 Francis sang : **On that day the Lord sent.** . . . Verse 6 echoes: **This is the day the Lord has made.** . . . And for Francis, only exultation and gladness are appropriate on such a **day**:

**6. This is the day the Lord has made;
let us exult and be glad in it.**
   [Ps 117:24]

As indicated in the structure of verse 5, verse 7 recalls the historical event of the Nativity and corresponds to

COMMENTARY

the manifestation of God's mercy, which is one of the major themes of the liturgy of Christmas:

- We receive, O God, *your mercy* . . .
- Show us, O Lord, *your mercy*. . . .
  (Matins, second nocturn)
- According to *his mercy*, he saved us . . .
  (Mass of Dawn, epistle)
- With the Lord is *mercy*. . . . (second Vespers).

Would this not be God's answer to the request expressed each Sunday of Advent at the hour of Sext: "*Show us*, O Lord, *your mercy* and grant us your salvation"?

This meeting of **mercy** and *sweetness* has overtones to Francis' interpretation of his experience of conversion when the Lord led him among lepers whose very sight he always avoided out of disgust:

> I experienced **mercy** with them. And when I took leave from them, that which appeared bitter to me was changed for me into *sweetness* of soul and body.
> [Test 2–3]

In PsF 15 Francis expresses God's answer to humanity's call for mercy in the following manner:

> 7. **For the most holy beloved child**
>   **is given to us,**
>   **and he was born for us along the way**
>   **and placed in a manger**
>   **because he had no place at the inn.**
>   [Is 9:6; Lk 2:7, 12, 16]

As he already did in verse 4, Francis makes significant changes to the material used to compose verse 7. His

Psalm 15

starting point is the opening antiphon of the Christmas Day Mass, a text adapted from the prophet Isaiah:

> A child is born *(natus est)* unto us,
> a son is given *(datus est)* to us.

This he combined with quotations from Luke's Nativity narrative to create a text which, taken literally, would read:

> For the most holy beloved Child
>   *is* given *(datus **est**)* to us,
> and he *was* born *(natus **fuit**)* for us. . . .

Since Isaiah's text was most likely well known to Francis, the change in the verb tense (from "*is* born" to "*was* born") can only be deliberate, allowing him to stress thereby the fact that the gift of the **most holy beloved Child** is an ever present grace (**is born**), whereas his birth is a once-and-for-all, historically dated event (**was born**).

Other changes in the quoted texts occur in the second half of verse 7. In his gospel, Luke writes, according to the common version of the time: "(Mary) gave birth to a son, her first born. . . and *laid (reclinavit)* him in manger, for there was no place for *them (eis)* at the inn" [Lk 2:7]. Francis first replaces the expression "*laid* in a manger" with **placed in a manger**, taken from the "sign" the angel gave the shepherds: "You will find an infant, wrapped in swaddling clothes and **placed *(positum)* in a manger**" [Lk 2:12]. He thereby creates a significant contrast, namely, the infant which is here **placed in a manger** is the One whom the Father **placed as the first born, the highest above the kings of the earth** as pro-

COMMENTARY

claimed at the conclusion of the first quatrain above [PsF 15:4].

This contrast between the lowliness of the Hero's birth and the majesty of his final state is further accentuated by another change Francis brings to Luke's text and which concentrates the attention on the Child: **he had** *(habebat)* **no place at the inn** instead of "*there was (erat)* no place *for them (eis)* at the inn." Here Francis likely got his cue from his Gospel Lectionary, which his companion Leo had bound with Francis' breviary and gave to the monastery of the Poor Clares in Assisi where it is still kept. The version found in this book reads: "there was no place for *him (ei)* at the inn." Francis may be suggesting a subtle twist to his interpretation of this text in the sense that the inn was not an appropriate place for someone who had chosen poverty. The manger was!

Finally, Francis notes that it was **along the way** that the **beloved** [cf. Mt 17:5] **Child was born for us**. This interesting detail comes most likely from a homily of St. Gregory read during Matins at Christmas and in which the homilist explains that the Lord "is not born in his parents' house, but **along the way**, to show that in assuming his humanity, he would be born, as it were, in an alien land." Such an image sets the stage for the Hero's situation in his geste as **stranger** and **pilgrim** [PsF 5:8] and for his dramatic call in the final moments on the cross to **all who pass along the way** [PsF 6:1].

The last verse [v. 8] of this second quatrain was announced in verse 5 by these words: **and at night (the Lord sent) his song**. And this is the Christmas song *par excellence*, since it was sung by the multitude of angels

Psalm 15

on the night of the Hero's birth and frequently repeated in the liturgies of the Christmas season:

> **8. Glory to the Lord God in the highest and on earth peace to men of good will.**
> [Lk 2:14]

With the Christmas liturgy, Francis hailed his Hero as the "*Peaceful* King" and sang of the "real *peace* which from heaven descends to us," of "the abundance of *peace*" which "rises on the day of the Lord." And every day of the year at Lauds, he celebrated in the Canticle of Zechariah "the Child who will be called Prophet of the Most High," "dawn from on high" and who will "illumine those who sit in darkness and in the shadow of death, to guide our footsteps **along the way** of **peace**." As a disciple of this "*peaceful* King," Francis strove to be counted among the **men of good will** and considered peace-making an essential part of his life commitment.

Thus ends the second quatrain of Francis' Christmas song with the heavenly proclamation of messianic peace.

*

The first verse of the third quatrain [v. 9] returns to the opening call of this Christmas psalm (**Exult in God...**) and invites all of creation (**all the earth**) to join the angels' song. The material of this third section and the sequence in which it is presented come from Ps 95 (**Sing to** the Lord **a new song . . .**) and its antiphon (**Let heavens rejoice . . .**) which were prayed during the third nocturn of Christmas Matins. But Francis made

COMMENTARY

deliberate choices in Ps 95, most likely to respect the quatrain structure of his Christmas song:

PsF 15: 9	=	Antiphon (+Ps 95:11–12a)
PsF 15:10	=	Ps 95:1
PsF 15:11	=	Ps 95:4
PsF 15:12	=	Ps 95:7.

At first, Francis probably used only the antiphon for his verse 9, which would explain the slight change he made in verse 10 of his psalm:

- verse 9 [Antiphon]
  Let heavens rejoice and the earth exult
  before the face of the Lord for he comes.

- verse 10 [Ps 95:1]
  Sing to him (instead of "to the Lord") **a new song** . . .

But at a later date he replaced the text of the antiphon with Ps 95:11–12a which begins with the same words: **Let heavens rejoice and the earth exult**. And he obviously made this change because he wanted a text that would include all of creation:

9. **Let heavens rejoice and earth exult,**
   the sea and all that is in it be moved,
   let fields and all that is in them be glad.
   [Ps 95:11–12a]

Then comes an invitation to continue to sing the **new song** which the angels had first sung:

10. **Sing to him a new song;**
    sing to the Lord, all the earth!
    [Ps 95:1]

Psalm 15

This last quatrain of Francis' Christmas song, although structured from material taken from the Christmas liturgy, is, nevertherless, more aligned with the spirit of Epiphany, the Hero's first manifestation to all nations. Traditionally this was highlighted by the visit of the Magi who, in Francis' time, were already looked upon as three kings representing the peoples of the earth. In verse 12, the expression **Bring to the Lord**, repeated three times, suggests the processional offerings of the three kings to **the Lord** who is **highly to be praised** and, although just born, already **worthy of awe**, **above all** the **gods** worshipped by the various peoples of the earth:

11. **For the Lord is great
    and highly to be praised;
    worthy of awe above all gods.**
    [Ps 95:4]

12. **Bring to the Lord, families of nations,
    bring to the Lord glory and honor,
    bring to the Lord the glory due his name.**
    [Ps 95:7–8a]

*

In the first quatrain of PsF 15, Francis situated the Hero's birth in the wider context of his saving mission. In the final dismissal verse, Francis recalls some of the attitudes and behaviors which flow from the Christmas event and witness to it:

- rejection of the "body" (the sinful self);
- continuation of Simon of Cyrene's assistance;

COMMENTARY

- perseverance in the love of God and of companion-pilgrims **on the way** [cf. PsF 7:8]:

    13. **Reject your bodies
    and take up his holy cross;
    and follow his most holy commands
    even to the end.**
    [Ps 95:8b; Mt 16:24; 10:22; cf. Jn 15:10]

***

Francis' Christmas song is somewhat like a triptych illustrating:

- the Hero's heavenly origin and equality with the Father (first quatrain);
- his humble virginal birth which is nevertheless acclaimed by heavenly choirs (second quatrain);
- his prophetic manifestation to the nations of the earth (third quatrain).

PsF 15 is the last psalm of Francis' Little Office. However, it is the prelude to what can be called Francis' "symphony for a Hero":

1. the Hero's geste [PsF 1–7];
2. its thematic variations and complementary motifs [PsF 8–13];
3. the vision of its final fulfillment in the Kingdom of God [PsF 14].

Postlude

The Prelude which introduced the commentaries of Francis' psalms suggested that they could be compared to a musical composition with a main theme—the story line of the Hero's geste, with variations and complementary motifs. On the basis of what we know of Francis' reference material (the liturgy, his *Breviary and Gospel Book*, church iconography, epic songs—the geste*s*—and theater), the commentaries represent an effort to read his texts as a window on his vision of the world and on his experience of the gospel message.

Inspired above all by the gospel according to John, Francis' psalms subtly weave archetypal images with basic human references and experiences, setting the stage for his Hero's great geste of cosmic dimension and consequence:

- his being sent on mission by the most holy Father of heaven;
- his humble birth along the way as a pilgrim and stranger;
- his zeal for the Father's house—all of creation—plunged into ruin by the cunning of the Enemy;
- his encounters with the Enemy, the Prince of this world;
- his steadfast hope in the Father throughout his entire mission;
- his final body-to-body combat with the Enemy on the cross;

- the disclosure of the ultimate significance of his ignominious elevation on the cross: his exaltation in the glory of the most holy Father in heaven and his enthronement as great King over all the earth;
- his commissioning of his disciples to witness to the Good News of his victory over darkness, deceit, despair and death;
- and the proclamation of his return to bring creation to its final stage of completion, including the judgment of the false justice that condemns the just and the permanent establishment of all God's children in the unity of the heavenly Jerusalem, where they will forever share in the fullness of the life he now experiences.

As "herald of the Great King," Francis refined his geste over a period of many years. And yet it remains an unfinished symphony. Had he lived longer and continued to transform his psalms according to the rhythm of his contemplation, we would still be left with an unfinished work since the very object of his contemplation—the Father's plan for creation and the role assumed therein by Francis' Hero—is fathomless by nature. But by its very incompleteness, Francis' *Little Office of the Passion*, and his psalms in particular, offers a path which can introduce one to his compelling experience of the Good News. Therein no doubt lies the secret of the fascination the Poverello still exercises eight hundred years after his passage from this world to the Father, in the footsteps of Christ, his Hero.

Printed in January 2001
Stamperia Editrice Commerciale
Bergamo
Italy